Lydia Schumacher
From Eternal to Everlasting

CHRONOI
Zeit, Zeitempfinden, Zeitordnungen
Time, Time Awareness, Time Management

Edited by
Eva Cancik-Kirschbaum, Christoph Markschies and
Hermann Parzinger

on behalf of the Einstein Center Chronoi

Volume 19

Lydia Schumacher

From Eternal to Everlasting

God and Time in Franciscan Thought

DE GRUYTER

ISBN 978-3-11-914902-0
e-ISBN (PDF) 978-3-11-170542-2
e-ISBN (EPUB) 978-3-11-170583-5
ISSN 2701-1453
DOI https://doi.org/10.1515/9783111705422

This work is licensed under the Creative Commons Attribution-NonCommercial-NoDerivatives 4.0 International License. For details go to https://creativecommons.org/licenses/by-nc-nd/4.0.

Library of Congress Control Number: 2025945626

Bibliographic information published by the Deutsche Nationalbibliothek
The Deutsche Nationalbibliothek lists this publication in the Deutsche Nationalbibliografie; detailed bibliographic data are available on the internet at http://dnb.dnb.de.

© 2026 with the author(s), published by Walter de Gruyter GmbH, Berlin/Boston, Genthiner Straße 13, 10785 Berlin.
This book is published with open access at www.degruyterbrill.com.

www.degruyterbrill.com
Questions about General Product Safety Regulation:
productsafety@degruyterbrill.com

For Johannes
With all my love

Acknowledgements

I am incredibly grateful to the directors of the Einstein Chronoi Center, Christoph Markschies and Eva Cancik-Kirschbaum, for the opportunity to hold a fellowship, which allowed me to work on this book in Berlin during the summer of 2023. I am also profoundly grateful to the staff at the Chronoi – in particular, Stefanie Rabe, Cinzia Pappi, and Felix Weidemann, for tirelessly supporting my research, especially when the plans for my fellowship had to be re-arranged to accommodate my pregnancy and maternity leave. I owe an especially big debt of thanks to Stefanie Rabe, for carefully copy editing my final manuscript, and to Yosef Elharar for gathering library books and scanning reading materials for me during the summer of 2023 when I was in the third trimester of my pregnancy.

More generally, I am grateful for and will always remember fondly the warm and welcoming academic community that the staff and directors fostered at the Chronoi, and the friendships with colleagues that I formed there. The time spent at the center in Berlin will definitely remain one of the highlights of my career, not least because it will always be linked with the birth of my son Christian in Berlin – the very first 'Chronoi baby'! Last but not least, I am hugely grateful to four colleagues who offered expert feedback on this manuscript at various points in its development: Claus Anderson, Oleg Bychkov, Gloria Frost, and Zita Toth. Their comments were crucial in helping me improve the manuscript.

I would like to dedicate this volume to my husband, Johannes Zachhuber – a dedication which does not however begin to do justice to you or to my love and admiration for you or to the happiness that you have brought into my life and that we share together.

Contents

Acknowledgements —— VII

Introduction —— 1

The Divine Nature: Simple or Infinite? —— 7
    Classical Simplicity: Augustine, Boethius, and Anselm —— 8
    Peter Lombard —— 11
    Richard of St Victor —— 13
    Alan of Lille —— 16
    Alexander of Hales —— 18
    The *Summa Halensis* —— 19

The Divine Nature: Eternal or Everlasting? —— 22
    Augustine —— 22
    Boethius —— 26
    Anselm of Canterbury —— 28
    Alan of Lille —— 30
    Peter Lombard —— 30
    Alexander of Hales —— 32
    The *Summa Halensis* —— 35

Metaphysical Foundations in Avicenna and the *Summa Halensis* —— 39
    Avicenna's *Metaphysics* —— 40
    Avicenna's Metaphysics in the *Summa Halensis* —— 42
    Possible Worlds —— 45
    Avicenna and the *Summa Halensis* on Eternity —— 48
    Aristotle and Avicenna on the Eternity of the World —— 49
    The *Summa Halensis* on The Eternity of the World —— 51

Time in Avicenna and the Franciscan Tradition —— 54
    Aristotle on Time —— 54
    Avicenna on Time —— 56
    The *Summa Halensis* on Time —— 60
    Later Franciscan Accounts of Time —— 66
    Conclusion —— 80

God's Knowledge of Future Contingents —— 84
        The *Summa Halensis* on Future Contingents —— 84
        John Duns Scotus on Future Contingents —— 88
        Ockham on Future Contingents —— 94
        Modern Views of God's Everlasting Nature —— 98
        Conclusion —— 99

Bibliography —— 102

Index of Names —— 109

Index of Subjects —— 110

Introduction

Among modern theologians and philosophers, the notion of God as everlasting has been considered essential to accounting for God's ability to interact with human beings in time and thus to affirming the nature of God as presented in the Bible.[1] For most contemporary thinkers, God's everlastingness entails that he is somehow subject to the flow of time, even though he is usually conceived as a being who lacks a beginning or end and thus does not share the same limitations as temporal creatures.[2] So construed, the idea of God as everlasting stands in sharp contrast to the notion that he is timelessly eternal – a being who is completely outside of time and not in any way subject to temporal categories.

This latter view prevailed for much of antiquity and continued to be defended in the Middle Ages by Latin Christian authorities like Augustine, Boethius, and Anselm. However, it has been less frequently advocated by modern scholars, who have been inclined to see it as depicting a God who is too distant from or uninvolved with his creatures in time.[3] The present work traces the shift from this medieval 'majority view' of God as eternal in favour of a more moderate idea of God's everlasting nature – one which does not go so far as to see God as subject to temporal changes but nonetheless allows for some correspondence of temporal categories to God.

This kind of idea was advocated particularly clearly by members of the Franciscan order, which was founded by Francis of Assisi in the early thirteenth century with a view to bringing God's message of redemption to all people and his love to the poor and downtrodden of society. Not long after its initial establishment, members of the order began to congregate in cities, where their ministry could have the greatest impact. The city of Paris posed a particular attraction for the friars, in that it had become the leading centre for theological study during

---

[1] See for example Ryan T. Mullins, *The End of the Timeless God* (Oxford: Oxford University Press, 2016). Richard Sorabji, *Time, Creation and the Continuum: Theories in Antiquity and the Early Middle Ages* (London: Duckworth, 1983).

[2] Many if not most modern theologians prefer the idea that God is everlasting to the traditional doctrine of eternity, favoring the view that God is subject in some way to time even though he does not have the same limitations as temporal beings. See for example Richard Swinburne, 'Eternal and Immutable,' in *The Coherence of Theism* (Oxford: Clarendon Press, 1977), 228–44. Keith Ward, *God: A Guide for the Perplexed* (London: OneWorld Publishers, 2002). See also e.g. John Polkinghorne, Wolfhart Pannenberg, John Macquarrie. Thomas F. Torrance, Jürgen Moltmann, and process theologians like Alfred North Whitehead and Charles Hartshorne.

[3] Brian Leftow, *Time and Eternity* (Ithaca: Cornell University Press, 2009). Eleonore Stump and Norman Kretzmann, 'Eternity,' *The Journal of Philosophy* 78:8 (August 1981), 429–58.

the twelfth century and witnessed the establishment of the first university theology faculty around 1200.

One of the masters at this faculty, Alexander of Hales, entered the Franciscan order in 1236 and became regent master of the Franciscan school in Paris, where he worked closely with other Franciscan scholars, especially John of La Rochelle, to compose a massive *Summa* of distinctly Franciscan theological and philosophical positions between 1236–56. The so-called *Summa Halensis* quickly became the basis for the theological education of Franciscan friars in the thirteenth-century university. Moreover, it distinguished the Franciscan school from others that existed at the time, such as the one that originated shortly thereafter in the work of the famous Dominican, Thomas Aquinas.

While Aquinas preserved the classical idea of God as timelessly eternal, the authors of the *Summa Halensis* initiated the trend in conceiving God's eternal nature in terms of his everlasting or infinite duration. According to my argument, two main factors influenced the development of this novel doctrine. The first was a more theological influence 'from above', namely, a new emphasis on divine infinity and so correspondingly on God's infinite or everlasting duration. The second main influence came 'from below', that is, from philosophical sources and especially the theory of time that was formulated by the medieval Islamic philosopher, Avicenna (Ibn Sina; 980–1037).

As recent scholarship has shown, Avicenna served as the main mediator of the Aristotelian tradition in the early thirteenth century, when the founders of the Franciscan school were flourishing.[4] Although many of Aristotle's own works were translated from Greek and available in the West by the mid-to-late twelfth century, a good number of those translations were initially incomplete or considered unreliable. The appearance around 1230 in Paris of a complete translation of Aristotle's major works from Arabic, alongside the commentaries on Aristotle by Averroes, provided a new opportunity to engage with his thinking. Nevertheless, the trend in appropriating Aristotle still took time to catch on, and it was not until Thomas Aquinas commissioned revised Latin translations from the Greek in the 1260's that Aristotle became a leading authority for university scholars.

From this point, Aristotle's reception became the phenomenon with which medieval scholasticism was most closely associated, as it has been by modern

---

[4] Amos Bertolacci, 'On the Latin Reception of Avicenna's Metaphysics before Albertus Magnus: An Attempt at Periodization,' in *The Arabic, Hebrew and Latin Reception of Avicenna's Metaphysics*, ed. Dag Nikolaus Hasse, Amos Bertolacci (Berlin: De Gruyter, 2012), 197–223. Dag Nikolaus Hasse, *Avicenna's* De anima *in the Latin West: The Formation of a Peripatetic Philosophy of the Soul 1160–1300* (London: The Warburg Institute, 2000).

scholars. Prior to the mid thirteenth century, however, Latin thinkers drew much more heavily on their own Latin Christian sources, such as Augustine, Boethius, and Anselm, and increasingly also on recently-translated works by Greek Christian authors like Pseudo-Dionysius and John of Damascus. The writings of these figures exhibited a strongly Neo-Platonic bent that was also found albeit in a highly unique and original form in Avicenna's writings. Thus, Avicenna made it possible to provide a sophisticated philosophical interpretation of Christian Neo-Platonic sources such as Augustine while reconciling them with the newly discovered aspects of the Aristotelian tradition. The incorporation of Avicenna's thinking on time as well as the metaphysical principles that underpinned it is ultimately what I will argue enabled Franciscans to redefine the eternalist tradition that dominated previous Latin thought.

To illustrate how they did so, chapter 1 ('The Divine Nature: Simple or Infinite?') will start by tracing the changes in understanding God's relationship to time that resulted from a more fundamental theological shift in thinking about the basic nature of God. Although early Franciscans continued to speak of God as simple, as was traditional amongst advocates of divine timelessness, they redefined the meaning of simplicity in accordance with their commitment to describing infinity as the essential feature of the divine nature. As we will see, multiple sources, including Avicenna, helped encourage thinking about God as infinite. The twelfth-century thinker Richard of St Victor also stands out as a particularly important influence for early Franciscans in this connection.

The second chapter ('The Divine Nature: Eternal or Everlasting?') will turn to consider the impact that a preference for describing God as simple or infinite had on the way he was conceived as eternal. As we will see, proponents of simplicity, such as Augustine, Boethius, and Anselm, denied that God knows the past and future as such and argued instead that he sees all times as instantaneously present from his own eternal perspective. On this basis, they argued that God is timeless. By contrast, the early Franciscan emphasis on infinity encouraged a tendency to conceive of God's eternity in terms of his infinite duration, that is, his existence at and knowledge of all times, past, present or future.

In chapter 3 ('Metaphysical Foundations in Avicenna and the *Summa Halensis*'), the philosophical influence of Avicenna will be drawn out more explicitly as a key factor underlying this shift in thinking about the precise sense in which God is 'eternal', even though early Franciscan theologians stretched his views considerably in bringing their changes about. In particular, this chapter will show how Avicenna's signature metaphysical distinction between necessary and possible beings allowed early Franciscans to develop an account of God as the infinite source of all finite possible beings which in turn supported the view of him as a being of infinite duration.

Following this discussion, chapter 4 ('The Nature of Time in Avicenna and the *Summa Halensis*') will focus on more specific evidence for Avicenna's influence 'from below' on the Summa's understanding of time, and consequently, eternity. As I will show, Avicenna's view of time departed quite sharply from the otherwise dominant theory of Aristotle, who developed what has been described as a 'static' theory, in which time represents the distance between two temporal points, namely, before and after. By contrast, Avicenna articulated what has been described as a 'dynamic' account of 'flowing' time, which is characterized by a constant movement of the present from the future into the past.

These two different ways of conceiving time can be usefully categorized, respectively, according to a typology famously presented by John M. Ellis McTaggart, who distinguished between an A-series or a B-series of time.[5] The B-series type construes temporal events as earlier and later than one another. The events that occur in a B-series are not therefore subject to change, because they always stand in the same relationship to one another, i.e. as earlier or later.[6] This is arguably how Aristotle conceived time, namely, as the space that intervenes between certain earlier and later moments. By contrast, the A-series that can be associated with Avicenna presupposes the categories of past, present, and future which are always in a state of flux with respect to one another. In that sense, the A-series regards past, present, and future as real, whereas the present alone is real in a B-series.

Following the discussion of Avicenna's temporal theory, chapter 4 will further show how the *Summa Halensis* formulates a similar position on time. I will then trace the subsequent development of its views through later Franciscans like John Duns Scotus (d. 1308) and William of Ockham (1287–1347), who helped draw the theory to its logical conclusion, namely, that time is akin to motion. This discussion will ultimately help to illuminate why Franciscans preferred to speak of God as a being of infinite duration rather than as timeless. Although Franciscans continued to locate God outside of time and denied that he is subject to temporal progression, their emphasis on God's everlasting nature allowed them to affirm more strongly the respects in which temporal moments are present to God precisely in terms of their temporality – as past, present, or future – rather than simply viewed simultaneously from the perspective of his 'eternal now'.

This becomes clear and is elaborated in chapter 5 ('God's Knowledge of Future Contingents'), which explores how Franciscan views of time and eternity effected

---

[5] John M. Ellis McTaggart, 'The Unreality of Time,' *Mind* 689 (1908), 457–74. See also McTaggart's, *The Nature of Existence,* vol. 2 (Cambridge: Cambridge University Press, 1927).
[6] McTaggart, 'The Unreality of Time,' 458.

their understanding of the manner in which God knows future contingents – events which have not yet occurred but may take place in the future. On this topic, early Franciscans argued that God has the ability to know the future and indeed all temporal categories in virtue of his knowledge of himself as the cause of all things, both those that are and those that will be. Duns Scotus agreed with the Summists on some level that God's knowledge of himself as the cause of all things entails an understanding of how creatures are related to him in time. However, he insisted that this knowledge requires the actual existence of the creature which is the object divine knowledge. On this basis, Scotus denies that God can know the future until it comes to pass. Otherwise, Scotus states that God would render future events necessary and thus undermine the freedom of the will.

In order to avoid this outcome, Scotus devised an innovative solution according to which God knows what will happen in the future only by inspecting the contents of the divine will, which determines what God will eventually allow or cause to come to pass. On his understanding, the divine will is by definition contingent. In other words, it can will something to be true or false at the same time, leaving both options entirely open up until the moment of willing. For this reason, God's foreknowledge of the future through his knowledge of his own divine will does not undermine the contingency of the future or human freedom.

William of Ockham later contested this conclusion on the grounds that the involvement of the divine will in determining future contingents would in fact undermine free will. In order to preserve the contingency of the future, Ockham concluded that God cannot strictly speaking know future contingents at all – or at least we cannot know how he knows them – until they actually come to pass. In that sense, God is subject as we are to the discoveries that take place in time, even though he himself is not a temporal being.

From a theological and even biblical point of view, this outlook has advantages, in that it lays an emphasis on God's intimate awareness of temporal affairs, which the account of God as timeless might seem to obscure.[7] At the same time, however, those who hold that God is timelessly eternal might argue that describing God as infinite in duration or everlasting – at least in the way Ockham seemingly did so – undermines God's absolute transcendence and his ability to know all things. In the present context, my task is not necessarily to adjudicate the theological strengths and weaknesses of each position.

Instead, my aim is to show how the notion of God as everlasting entered into the stream of Western Christian thought and the sources and factors – both the-

---

7 The strengths and weaknesses of the sempiternal account are discussed by John L. Tomkinson, 'Divine Sempiternity and Atemporality,' *Religious Studies* 18 (1982), 177–89.

ological or 'from above' and philosophical or 'from below' – that shaped it in the process. In this way, I help to reveal how it could eventually become a dominant strand in the contemporary understanding of God. At the same time, however, I highlight how the early Franciscan approach particularly emerges as an apt resource for tempering some of the more extreme variations of the theory which go so far as to attribute to God temporal qualities which only seem befitting to creatures. In that sense, the early Franciscan idea of God as everlasting provides a sort of 'middle way' between the theories of God as timelessly eternal or everlasting to the point of being actually subject to the flow of time.

The Divine Nature: Simple or Infinite?

At the start of the scholastic period, theologians generally described God's nature as essentially simple, following a longstanding Western tradition that stemmed from the great Church Father Augustine (354–430) and was further elaborated by later Christian thinkers like Boethius (d. 524) and Anselm (d. 1109). As recent research has demonstrated, however, the period witnessed a gradual transition as a result of which many theologians began to describe God's nature as primarily infinite.[1] Although earlier theologians had also spoken of God's infinity, they generally followed the Latin Church Father Hilary of Poitiers (315–67) in defining it as a feature of God's power, which is manifested in creation but is capable of much more than what is observed there.[2] Additionally, scholastics linked infinity with divine eternity, that is, God's freedom from temporal constraints.

The new focus on infinity as the primary feature of God's nature was precipitated by a number of factors, first and foremost, the introduction of Greek patristic texts by figures like John of Damascus (c. 675–749) and Pseudo-Dionysius (5th/6th c.), who spoke of God as an infinite and incomprehensible being. As I will show below, the twelfth-century theologians Richard of St Victor (1110–73) and Alan of Lille (1128–1202/3) also undertook new discussions of divine infinity, which influenced early scholastic theologians, who in turn sought to reconcile the newly translated Greek sources with their own longstanding Augustinian tradition.[3]

The Franciscan thinkers who flourished in the early thirteenth century found the notion of divine infinity particularly attractive, because it allowed them to stress the close relationship between the finite and the infinite – the direct knowa-

---

[1] This section on God as infinite or simple draws on a chapter on 'The Divine Nature,' by Lydia Schumacher in *The Origins of Scholasticism at the University of Paris: Theology and Philosophy in Paris 1150–1250* (Cambridge: Cambridge University Press, 2025), 183–207. Antoine Côté, *L'infinité divine dans la théologie médiévale (1220–1255)* (Paris: Vrin, 2002). Anne Ashley Davenport, *Measure of a Different Greatness: The Intensive Infinite, 1250–1650* (Leiden: Brill, 1999). Leo Sweeney, S.J., 'Divine Infinity: 1150–1250,' *The Modern Schoolman* 35 (November 1957), 38–51.
[2] Sweeney, 'Divine Infinity: 1150–1250,' 42, citing Hilary of Poitiers, *De Trinitate*, 1.4, 5, ed. Hugo Hurter, *Sancti Hilarii Pictaviensis Episcopi De Trinitate Libri* (Oeniponti: Libraria Academica Wagneriana, 1887); see the translation by Stephen McKenna in, *Saint Hilary of Poitiers: The Trinity*, in *The Fathers of the Church*, vol. 25 (Washington, D.C.: Catholic University of America Press, 1954).
[3] Hyacinthe-François Dondaine, 'L'objet et le "medium" de la vision béatifique chez les théologiens du XIIIe siècle,' *Recherches de théologie ancienne et médiévale* 19 (1952), 60–130.

bility of God through finite beings and his care for each and every one of them.[4] By contrast, advocates of divine simplicity, most famously in the high Middle Ages, Thomas Aquinas, expressly denied the possibility of knowing God through creatures, insisting that these can only afford 'negative' knowledge of what God is not, namely, limited, temporal, and so on, thus reinforcing the sense that God himself far exceeds all that we are capable of knowing.

Whereas proponents of simplicity saw God as timelessly eternal, those who advocated infinity began to conceive of him as infinite in terms of his duration. In a sense, then, they understood God as everlasting, even though most medieval thinkers continued to use the language of eternity in speaking about God. To discern their reasons for doing so, it will help to trace the basic lines of the transition from simplicity to infinity through some of the key early scholastic players in the discussion, including Peter Lombard (1100–60), Alan of Lille, Richard of St Victor, Alexander of Hales (1185–1245), and ultimately, the *Summa Halensis*. As noted already, this text was overseen by Alexander of Hales after he became a Franciscan friar in 1236, but was co-authored by several other Franciscans, most importantly, John of La Rochelle (d. 1245). As noted already, this Summa represents the first major attempt to outline the contours of a distinctly Franciscan point of view.

Classical Simplicity: Augustine, Boethius, and Anselm

The classic statement of the doctrine of divine simplicity can be found in figures like Augustine, Boethius, and Anselm of Canterbury, who are justifiably regarded as its most distinguished early medieval champions. In his *City of God*, Augustine articulates the view clearly while linking it to God's immutability. As he states: there is 'a good which alone is simple and, therefore, which alone is unchangeable, and this is God. This good has created all goods; but these are not simple and, therefore, they are mutable.'[5] The contrast between mutable and immutable beings is one Augustine draws out further in his mature theological treatise, *De Trinitate*:[6]

---

[4] Jacob W. Wood, 'Kataphasis and Apophasis in Thirteenth Century Theology: The Anthropological Context of the *Triplex Via* in the *Summa fratris Alexandri* and Albert the Great,' *The Heythrop Journal* 57 (2016), 293–311.

[5] Augustine, *The City of God Books VIII-XVI*, 11.10, trans. Gerald G. Walsh, Grace Monahan, in *The Fathers of The Church*, vol. 14 (Washington, D.C.: The Catholic University of America Press, 1952), 202; John P. Rosheger, 'Augustine and Divine Simplicity,' *New Blackfriars* 77:901 (1996), 72–83.

[6] Augustine, *The Trinity*, 5.1–2, trans. Stephen McKenna, in *The Fathers of The Church*, vol. 45 (Washington, D.C.: The Catholic University of America Press, 1963), 175–77.

> All other things that are called essences or substances are susceptible of accidents, by which a change, whether great or small, is brought about in them. But there can be no accidents of this kind in God. Therefore, only the essence of God, or the essence which God is, is unchangeable. Being is in the highest and truest sense of the term proper to Him from whom being derives its name. For what undergoes a change does not retain its own being, and what is subject to change, even though it may not actually be changed, can still lose the being which it had. And, therefore, only that which is not only not changed, but cannot undergo any change at all, can be called being in the truest sense without any scruple.[7]

As Augustine construes it here, God's essence is identical with his attributes. This means that he is not subject to change or limitations, such that he can become more or less wise, or be wise only in a particular way, like a human being. On this basis of such reasoning, Augustine concludes that names like 'Creator' which we give to God do not denote a change in his substance – i.e. that he 'became' a creator at the point of creation – but only indicate a change on the side of creatures, which come to exist in time through him at the moment of his initial creative act.[8] Likewise, when we say that God is angry with the unrighteous or merciful towards the good, this denotes a change on the human side, that is, in persons whose own behaviour affects their relation to God, rather than a change in God himself, who is always good. Thus, Augustine famously writes in his *Confessions* of the time in his life when he was estranged from God, 'you were with me, but I was not with you.'[9]

In his *Theological Tractates*, the great Roman philosopher Boethius formalizes Augustine's understanding of divine simplicity in discussing how the Aristotelian categories (substance, quantity, quality, relation, etc.) apply to creatures by contrast to God. On his account, such beings are not entirely what they are; a man for instance must mature and thus only has certain qualities like justice to a certain extent at any given point in time. These qualities are accidents in him, which he owes to something other than himself, i.e. to goodness, to wisdom, to justice.

By contrast, God's justice does not depend on anything else. For this reason, there is no qualification or limitation upon it. Rather, he is justice itself. As Boethius summarizes, 'God is simply and entirely God, for he is nothing else than what he is, and therefore he is, through simple existence.'[10] For Boethius, the fact that God is 'entirely himself' means that 'being and action are identical [in

---

7 Augustine, *The Trinity*, 5.2, trans. McKenna, 177.
8 Augustine, *The Trinity*, 5.16, trans. McKenna, 195–8.
9 Augustine, *Confessions*, 10.27.38, trans. Vernon J. Bourke, in *The Fathers of The Church*, vol. 21 (Washington, D.C.: The Catholic University of America Press, 1953), 297.
10 Boethius, *On the Trinity*, 4, in *Theological Tractates, De Consolatione Philosophiae*, trans. Hugo F. Stewart, Edward K. Rand, S. Jim Tester (Cambridge, MA: Harvard University Press, 1973), 19.

God; thus] to be good and to be just are one and the same for him. But being and action are not identical for us, for we are not simple. For us, then, goodness is not the same thing as justice.'[11]

In his *Monologion*, the Benedictine monk Anselm concurs with and renders even more precise the sentiments of his forebears concerning the simple nature of God. As he writes, 'the supreme essence is above and beyond all other natures.'[12] This is because 'all the other good things are good through something other than what they themselves are, while this thing alone is good through itself.'[13] For example, Anselm states, a horse can be good through swiftness or strength. However, God is good through himself and thus he is supremely good and the one being on account of whom all other beings have whatever form of goodness they may have.[14] For the same reason, God is the only being who exists through himself, and it is through him that all other beings exist.[15]

As such a being, God is not a composite of the qualities he possesses, such as goodness, justice, and so on; rather those different attributes are identical with and one with his essence and with each other.[16] The diversity of properties God may seem to exhibit, and which we ascribe to him, does not therefore strictly speaking apply to him as an ineffable being who 'transcends all human understanding.'[17] Rather, they arise from our own experiences which seem to suggest he is just, wise, etc. Thus, Anselm concludes that we must recognize that our conceptions of God's attributes fall short of and cannot capture his essence, which always exceeds what we can understand or articulate.

As Anselm elaborates, anything that is said of the 'supreme nature in respect of relation does not signify its substance. Hence the mere fact that the supreme nature is greater than everything that it has created clearly does not specify its natural essence. For it is called "greater" and "supreme" in relation to other things.'[18] Thus Anselm concludes that '"Supreme" therefore does not directly signify that essence which is, without qualification, greater and better than every-

---

[11] Boethius, *From the Same to the Same*, in *Theological Tractates, De Consolatione Philosophiae*, 51.
[12] Anselm of Canterbury, *Monologion*, 65, in *Anselm of Canterbury: The Major Works*, ed. Brian Davies, Gillian R. Evans (Oxford: Oxford University Press, 2008), 71.
[13] Anselm, *Monologion*, 1, ed. Davies/Evans, 13.
[14] Anselm, *Monologion*, 3, ed. Davies/Evans, 13–14.
[15] Anselm, *Monologion*, 3, ed. Davies/Evans, 14: 'Therefore, since all things exist through this one thing, beyond a shadow of a doubt this one thing exists through itself.'
[16] Anselm, *Monologion*, 17, ed. Davies/Evans, 30.
[17] Anselm, *Monologion*, 65, trans. Davies/Evans, 72.
[18] Anselm, *Monologion*, 15, trans. Davies/Evans, 26.

thing else.'[19] Rather, terms like 'supreme', like 'Lord' or 'Creator' reflect the relations that creatures have to God and the ways in which human beings understand him accordingly.

Peter Lombard

Peter Lombard was a pivotal figure in the medieval scholastic tradition, whose *Sentences*, written by around 1160, established the basic structure of theological inquiry which was followed in the universities for generations.[20] These *Sentences* were divided into four main volumes, which respectively cover the nature of God, creation, the Incarnation, and the Sacraments. Each volume was further subdivided according to many specific topics, on which the Lombard marshalled and commented upon quotations or 'sentences' from many authoritative sources, including the Bible and Church Fathers like Augustine and Hilary of Poitiers.

In writing commentaries on the *Sentences*, subsequent medieval thinkers expanded, contracted, and rearranged different aspects of Lombard's account, while broadly following the basic structure of Lombard's work. Although such commentaries were already written in the late twelfth and early thirteenth century, they had become by the 1240s the medieval equivalent to a doctoral thesis in theology which was required of every aspiring university master of theology.[21] Those masters who went on from this point to write *Summae*, such as Alexander of Hales and the authors of the *Summa Halensis*, tended to depart much more from the basic content and structure of the *Sentences* than the commentary genre would allow, while still covering many of the main topics the *Sentences* originally treated, including the doctrine of divine simplicity.

The Lombard's discussion of the simplicity of the divine essence falls within the broader account of the Trinity that he outlines in book 1 of the *Sentences.* Like many passages of his work, this one served as a *locus classicus* for subsequent thinkers who treated this same topic. Initially, Lombard links God's simplicity to his unchangeability, invoking a classic notion, which the Lombard traces to Jer-

---

19 Anselm, *Monologion*, 15, trans. Davies/Evans, 26.
20 Marcia L. Colish, *Peter Lombard*, 2 vols (Leiden: Brill, 1993). Philipp W. Rosemann, *Peter Lombard* (Oxford: Oxford University Press, 2004); idem., *The Story of a Great Medieval Book: Peter Lombard's Sentences* (Toronto: University of Toronto Press, 2007).
21 Nancy Spatz, 'Approaches and Attitudes to a New Theology Textbook: The *Sentences* of Peter Lombard,' in *The Intellectual Climate of the Early University: Essays in Honor of Otto Gründler,* ed. Nancy van Deusen (Kalamazoo: The Medieval Institute Publications, Western Michigan University, 1997), 27–52.

ome and Augustine, that God sees the past and future as present.[22] According to Lombard, this is because God is eternal and therefore always exists. By contrast to creatures, he cannot be described as an entity that 'was' or 'will be'.[23] To reinforce this claim, the Lombard quotes Hilary of Poitiers, who states that being or existence is not an accident in God, because it is identical with his essence.[24]

By contrast, Lombard observes, existence is accidental in temporal beings, because they not only began to exist but also cease to exist; thus, existence is not inseparable from their being. This is true of creaturely accidents more generally, which can be present in some beings and not in others and which have the potential to come and go or increase and decrease. As Lombard therefore stresses, accidents produce changes in creatures, whether great or small, which can never occur in God.[25] In his view, anything that is changed cannot serve as the cause of its own being but must be caused by another, namely, God, who is the cause of himself and all other beings.

Another significant difference between God and creatures that Lombard highlights concerns the fact that the latter are comprised of parts, the development and collaboration of which contribute to change, while the simple God is not.[26] In this connection, the Lombard acknowledges that the human soul might seem to be simple at least in comparison to the body, given that it does not have multiple parts but is wholly if virtually present in all the parts of the body through which it acts.[27] Nevertheless, the Lombard insists that the soul is not simple in the strict sense of the term, because it is subject to diverse passions, like fear, joy, and desire, as well as capacities, such as skilfulness, insightfulness.

All these features can be found in the soul independently of the others, or not at all, and they are in some souls more or less than in others. Moreover, they vary depending upon the feelings or inclinations of the soul at any given time.[28] On this basis, the Lombard concludes that the soul is not simple in the way of the divine, in whom 'there is no distinction between the one who possesses and the thing, which is possessed, as is the case in all other things. For the liquid's container

---

[22] Peter Lombard, *Magistri Petri Lombardi Parisiensis episcopi Sententiae in IV libris distinctae*, vol. 1 (Rome: Collegii S. Bonaventurae Ad Claras Aquas, 1971), 8.2.21, 95–96; trans. Giulio Silano, in *The Sentences: Book 1* (Toronto: Pontifical Institute of Medieval Studies, 2007). See also Lombard, *Sententiae*, 8.2.21, 98.
[23] Lombard, *Sententiae*, 2.18.6, 419–20.
[24] Lombard, *Sententiae*, 8.1.21, 96.
[25] Lombard, *Sententiae*, 1.8.2, 97–98.
[26] Lombard, *Sententiae*, 1.8.3–4, 98–99.
[27] Lombard, *Sententiae*, 1.8.3, 98.
[28] Lombard, *Sententiae*, 2.22.1, 439–40.

is not the liquid, and the body is not its colour, and the soul is not wisdom.'²⁹ By contrast, as previous proponents of divine simplicity had concluded, the various attributes of God's being, such as wisdom, justice, goodness, or truth, are identical with God's essence and signify who he unchangeably or indeed simply is.

In the context of defining God's simplicity, the Lombard briefly refers to God as infinite, although he does not clarify what he means by this. However, a quote from Hilary of Poitiers suggests that he sees God's infinity as a function of his eternity: God is infinite because he always exists.³⁰ The Lombard makes further reference to Hilary in discussing the power of God.³¹ Following Hilary, he argues that God's power is infinite or immeasurable so far as he is 'present everywhere and absent nowhere,'³² in creation, by which he is nonetheless not bounded.³³ As these brief references suggest, the Lombard takes a fairly traditional view of infinity as a feature of God's eternity or power or presence in the world – in sum, his unlimitedness by time or space. In all of these respects, however, infinity, does not represent the central attribute of the divine for the Lombard but is instead an outworking of his fundamentally simple nature.

Richard of St Victor

A key player in the Latin scholastic discussions of divine infinity or 'immensity' was Richard of St Victor, a younger contemporary of Hugh of St Victor (1096– 1141) who famously commented on and incorporated the works of Pseudo-Dionysius, popularizing them in the Parisian context where the School of St Victor was based. The notion of divine immensity comes to the fore in Richard's *De Trinitate*, which was probably written between 1162–73 and which significantly influenced the work of Alexander of Hales and subsequently the authors of the *Summa Halensis*.³⁴ At the outset of his account of the Trinity, Richard seeks to defend

---

29 Lombard, *Sententiae*, 1.8.28, 101–3.
30 Lombard, *Sententiae*, 1.8.8, 101, quoting Hilary, *De Trinitate*, 8.24; Sweeney, 'Divine Infinity: 1150–1250,' 43.
31 Sweeney, 'Divine Infinity: 1150–1250,' 41–42; Lombard, *Sententiae*, 1.43.1, 298.
32 Lombard, *Sententiae*, 1.37.1, 203, quoting Hilary, *De Trinitate*, 8.24.
33 Lombard, *Sententiae*, 1.37.1, 208.
34 Richard of St Victor, *De Trinitate: texte critique avec introduction, notes et tables*, ed. Jean Ribaillier (Paris: J. Vrin, 1958). See also the version of *De Trinitate*, in *Patrologia Latina*, vol. 196, ed. Jacques-Paul Migne (Paris, 1855). Translation by Ruben Angelici, *Richard of St Victor: On the Trinity* (Eugene: Cascade Books, 2011).

the claim that God is one and in particular to argue for the necessary existence of God and indeed only one God.[35]

Recently, scholarship has highlighted the similarities between Richard and Avicenna's arguments for the necessary existence of God, which will be discussed further in the section of this book dealing with Avicenna's metaphysics.[36] As Suf Amichay notes, Richard may have come across a simplified version of Avicenna's argument in the work of Gundissalinus (1115–90), who translated Avicenna's writings from Arabic into Latin.[37] This suggests that the early Franciscan authors received Avicennian ideas not only directly, through the works of Avicenna himself, but also indirectly, through Richard.

In order to argue that God exists necessarily, Richard appeals to a distinction found in Avicenna between beings that exist from themselves or from another – in other words, beings that cause their own existence or whose existence is caused by another being.[38] Richard deploys this distinction as the basis for identifying three different modes of being, which are mentioned in the work of John Scotus Eriugena (815–77), whose interest in Greek thought is well known, and whose translation of the Dionysian corpus would have been one of several available translations which Richard would likely have consulted.[39]

These modes of being are from eternity and deriving its existence from itself; neither from eternity nor from itself; or from eternity but not from itself. According to Richard, a fourth possibility – for a being that is from itself but not from eternity – is in fact impossible, because anything which is the cause of its own existence must always exist. Conversely, he claims, anything that is *not* the cause of its own existence cannot be eternal.[40]

---

[35] Richard of St Victor, *De Trinitate*, 1.5.

[36] Lydia Schumacher, 'The Proof for a Necessary Existent in the *Summa Halensis*,' in *The Summa Halensis: Doctrines and Debates*, ed. Lydia Schumacher (Berlin: De Grutyer, 2020), 59–72.

[37] Suf Amichay, 'Freedom and Plenitude in Medieval Arguments for the Existence of God' (PhD: Cambridge University, 2023), 117: 'There is no historical reason to reject the idea that Richard read Gundisallinus' book (*On the Procession of the World*), which was composed around 1160, before the earliest date Richard might have completed his book (*De Trinitate*), which ranges between 1162 to 1174. Furthermore, there is a strong reason to believe that Richard has read Gundisallinus' text, as his book offers some distinctly Avicennian ideas.'

[38] See especially Richard of St Victor, *De Trinitate*, 1.6.

[39] Richard of St Victor, *De Trinitate*, 1.8; cf. John Scotus Eriugena, *Divisione* I.1, 441b. Please note that the following material about Richard is published in another format in my article, 'The Early Franciscan Doctrine of Divine Immensity: Towards a Middle Way Between Classical Theism and Panentheism,' *Scottish Journal of Theology* 70:3 (2017), 278–94. See also my *Early Franciscan Theology: Between Authority and Innovation* (Cambridge: Cambridge University Press, 2019), 123–4.

[40] Richard of St Victor, *De Trinitate*, 1.7.

Such beings can only come into existence by virtue of a being that causes its own existence and is therefore eternal, namely, God.[41] Otherwise, there would be nothing from which beings that are unable to cause themselves could derive their being. In Richard's account, two such non-identical beings cannot exist, otherwise one would be superior to the other, and would not therefore be the greatest being from which all others derive.[42] On this basis, Richard concludes that there is only one God who exists necessarily, or from himself, and for that reason from eternity.[43]

In further inquiring about the meaning of eternity, Richard argues that God is everlasting in the sense that he has no beginning and no end.[44] He is also immutable and does not change.[45] In synthesizing these insights into one definition, Richard concludes that God is a being with no beginning or end who does not change and is therefore both everlasting *and* eternal. This we will see is a way of defining God's eternity that re-appears in the *Summa Halensis*, which does not however explicitly cite Richard in giving its definition of eternity. Nevertheless, Richard does not go as far as the Summa in affirming that God knows past and future as such but maintains the more traditional idea that he knows these times in virtue of his 'eternal now'.[46]

In this regard, Richard's own interest is in showing that a being that lacks either a beginning or an end is infinite. According to Richard however, a being that is infinite in terms of his eternity must also be so in virtue of his greatness, which cannot be measured in any way.[47] Here, Richard reiterates that there can only be one infinite or immense being, otherwise there would be multiple supreme beings, and as a result, neither would ultimately be supreme.[48] Such a supreme being cannot lack any desirable attributes, because his definition is to be all

---

41 Richard of St Victor, *De Trinitate*, 1.8.
42 Richard of St Victor, *De Trinitate*, 1.14–16.
43 Richard of St Victor, *De Trinitate*, 1.17.
44 Richard of St Victor, *De Trinitate*, 2.2.
45 Richard of St Victor, *De Trinitate*, 2.3–4.
46 Richard of St Victor, *De Trinitate*, 2.23, trans. Angelici, 109–10: 'He is also in every time with his eternity and in no [time] temporally. In fact, just as he who is simple and not composed [by multiple elements] cannot be distended in space, similarly, he who is eternal and unalterable cannot mutate in time. Thus, no reality that is still non-existent is future to him; in a similar manner, no reality that is no more is past to him; finally, no reality existing in the present is transitory to him.'
47 Richard of St Victor, *De Trinitate*, 2.5
48 Richard of St Victor, *De Trinitate*, 2.6.

that is good.⁴⁹ In that sense, Richard follows a longstanding tradition, upheld by Anselm, which posits the identity of God's essence and his attributes.⁵⁰

According to this tradition, we have seen that God is or is the same as the properties he has – he has them in their fullness – whereas creatures simply have those properties in limited or qualified ways. God is whatever it is best to be. As such, God is simple: not subject to the complex components or alterations that characterize his creatures.⁵¹ Richard thus concludes his discussion of divine infinity by seeking to reconcile it with the classical concept of divine simplicity. However, he initiates a noteworthy shift in describing infinity along with simplicity as a central feature of the divine essence or nature, not merely a property of the divine power. Another novel approach to infinity which proved influential for the *Summa Halensis* authors can be detected in the work of Richard's later contemporary, Alan of Lille, to whom we now turn.

Alan of Lille

Alan of Lille was another important figure in the early scholastic debate in Paris who along with Lombard – though perhaps not to the same degree – was heavily quoted by early theologians at the University of Paris, including the authors of the *Summa Halensis*.⁵² In his *Summa quoniam homines*, he makes a case for divine simplicity in the context of inquiring about the unity of the divine essence. His argument starts from the assumption that everything created is composed. According to Alan, there are three kinds of composition. One involves a composition of parts, such as is found in the human and other bodies. Another kind of composition concerns the composition of natures (*ex concretione naturarum*), according to which the soul is said to be composed, not because it is comprised of physical parts but because it is constituted of faculties like reason, memory, and intellect. A third kind of composition involves properties that are composed in their subjects.⁵³

According to Alan, whatever is composed and thus has a beginning to its existence must be caused by a being which has no beginning.⁵⁴ For nothing exists by

---

49 Richard of St Victor, *De Trinitate*, 2.16.
50 Richard of St Victor, *De Trinitate*, 2.10.
51 Richard of St Victor, *De Trinitate*, 2.20.
52 Côté, *L'infinité divine*, 18–22.
53 Alan of Lille, 'La Somme Quoniam Homines d'Alain de Lille,' ed. Palémon Glorieux, *Archives d'histoire doctrinale et littéraire du Moyen Âge* 20 (1953), 122.
54 Alan of Lille, 'La Somme,' 123.

chance, and nothing composes itself. Thus, Alan concludes that a being must have preceded compound things which composed them, and which is not itself composed but is entirely simple. Only such a being can be the cause of all things, because it is not preceded by another cause. There can only be one such being, on Alan's account.[55] For if there were numerous 'first causes', they would either possess the same properties or different ones, and thus there would be a composition of properties, and neither would be simple.

As an entirely simple being, Alan elaborates, God is identical with his properties like deity, incomprehensibility, and so on, for if his deity were something other to himself, there would be composition in God.[56] On the assumption that God is simple, Alan further infers that God is immense or immeasurable by both the senses and the intellect. As such, he is incomprehensible.[57] According to Alan, this is because he is not located in any specific place, although, as the efficient cause of all things, he is virtually present in all places.[58] Likewise, Alan states that God is infinite, because he is eternal and has no beginning or end in time.

For that reason, he is unbegotten, immutable and incorruptible: he does not come into being, change, or cease to be. On these grounds, Alan concludes that there are four ways in which God is infinite: in time, because he is eternal; in place, because he is immeasurable or immense; in kind, because he does not participate in any substantial form which would establish him as a finite kind of being; and also as regards the intellect, because he cannot be grasped.[59] As Coté has highlighted, this new typology of immensity/infinity, which Alan defines as aspects of God's simplicity, would end up shaping the stricture of the *Summa Halensis'* treatise on divine infinity, which notably differs from the personal account of Alexander of Hales, who oversaw the authorship of this text.[60]

---

55 Alan of Lille, 'La Somme,' 123
56 Alan of Lille, 'La Somme,' 134, cf. 141.
57 Alan of Lille, 'La Somme,' 123: 'Ex hiis etiam colligere possumus Deum esse immensum; quia cum sit simplex, remoto omni genere compositionis, tam compage partium quam concretione naturarum, eum nec metiri possumus mensura sensus nec mensura intellectus.'
58 Alan of Lille, 'La Somme,' 124: 'Deus enim immensus est, nec localis, nec locates quia ubique est, id est in omnibus rebus est tamquam efficiens causa, non ut loco distinguatur.'
59 Alan of Lille, 'La Somme,' 123–24: 'Ergo infinitus; quadruplici genere eternitatis: tempore, quia eternus; loco, quia immensus; genere quia cum nulla substantiali forma participet in nullo rerum genere sistitur; sola enim substantialis forma rem in certo genere constituit; ratione etiam intellectus, quia intellectu capi non potest, ut superius probatum est.'
60 Côté, *L'infinité divine*, 22.

Alexander of Hales

Before Alexander entered the Franciscan order in 1236, he had previously enjoyed a quite long and distinguished career as a theologian in the University of Paris. In this context, he championed the effort to introduce Lombard's *Sentences* as a basis alongside the Bible for teaching theology in the university and wrote one of the first glosses on the *Sentences*, thus helping to establish this genre as essential for any aspiring master of theology. While many of Alexander's own theological positions do ultimately feature in the *Summa Halensis*, there are cases where the ideas he developed in his personal works are jettisoned in favor of the contribution of other authors, especially John of La Rochelle, who likely composed volume 1 on the doctrine of God which includes the treatise on divine infinity.

The discussion of the divine nature in Alexander's Gloss on Lombard's *Sentences*, composed between 1221–27, is one example of this discrepancy with the text of the Summa in that it elaborates the more traditional view that God is simple.[61] For Alexander, as for Lombard, God's simplicity is closely linked with his eternity, the fact that he always exists and does not therefore transition from a state of non-being to being or vice versa.[62] The latter is the case for creatures, because they are from nothing. As a result, existence is an accident in creatures, which they can either lack or possess, depending on whether or not God causes them to exist and preserves them in being. For God, by contrast, existence is not an accident – or something that he receives from another entity – because he causes his own existence and that of all other beings.[63]

On this basis, Alexander affirms that essence and existence are the same in God (*in Deo, non differt esse et quod est*): there is no composition in him as there is in creatures, because he always is what he is, namely, being itself.[64] According to Alexander, there are numerous kinds of composition, for example, a composition of form with matter, or forms themselves, or parts, accidents or causes.[65] However, none of these types of composition can be found in God, whom Alexander further describes as immense or immeasurable in terms of his magnitude – that is, his power to produce infinite effects.[66]

---

[61] Alexander of Hales, *Magistri Alexandri de Hales Glossa in quatuor libros Sententiarum Petri Lombardi*, vol. 1 (Florence: Collegii S. Bonaventurae, 1951), 1.6, 100; Côté, *L'infinité divine*, 26–30.
[62] Alexander of Hales, *Glossa*, 1.8.10, 102.
[63] Alexander of Hales, *Glossa*, 1.8.28, 109.
[64] Alexander of Hales, *Glossa*, 1.8.10, 102.
[65] Alexander of Hales, *Glossa*, 1.8.20b, 105.
[66] Alexander of Hales, *Glossa*, 1.19.3, 192; cf. 1.19.29, 207.

According to Alexander, these effects do not render God spatially present or locally circumscribable in the world but only establish his virtual presence at all places and times.[67] In this connection, Alexander quotes a famous passage from Isidore of Seville's *De Trinitate*, which states: 'the immensity of the divine magnitude is such that we understand him to be inside all things, but not contained by them; outside all things, but not excluded from them.'[68] In light of this text, Alexander takes the standard view that the power of the divine essence is infinite.[69] For this same reason, he insists that God cannot be comprehended by the human mind, which is limited to the knowledge of finite things.[70] Thus, God's infinity is closely linked for Alexander not only to his omnipresence but also to his unknowability.[71]

The *Summa Halensis*

The tractate on divine immensity or infinity in the *Summa Halensis*, which was largely written between 1236–45, mostly likely by John of La Rochelle, moves beyond Alexander of Hales in championing these doctrines systematically for the first time. This text is certainly the longest on the subject from the period, running nearly fifty pages in the edition. It follows a much shorter section of just four pages which deals with the question of divine simplicity.[72] In this context, the Summist is mainly concerned with addressing the possible threat to simplicity that is posed by the multiple persons of the Trinity. The author does not therefore discuss any of the traditional aspects of the simplicity doctrine that have featured in the accounts discussed above and it quickly moves past this topic to treat the idea that God is essentially infinite.

Following the model established by Alan of Lille, the Summa divides its discussion of infinity into four sections on the immensity of God in himself, in relation to the human mind, in relation to location or space, as well as to time. The

---

67 Alexander of Hales, *Glossa*, 1.37.14, 370.
68 Alexander of Hales, *Glossa*, 1.37.39, 387: 'Isodorus, in libro *De Trinitate* "Immensitas divinae magnitudinis haec est, ut intelligamus eum intra omnia, non inclusum; extra omnia, non exclusum; et ideo interiorem ut omnia contineat, et exteriorem ut incircumscriptae suae magnitudinis immensitate omnia includat".'
69 Alexander of Hales, *Glossa*, 1.37.4d, 380: 'Sicut enim infinita est virtus divinae essentiae, sic finita est virtus uniuscuiusque creatae essentiae.'
70 Alexander of Hales, *Glossa*, 1.19,6.d, 193.
71 Côté, *L'infinité divine*, 28.
72 *Doctoris irrefragabilis Alexandri de Hales Ordinis minorum Summa theologica* (Quaracchi, Florentiae: Collegii S. Bonaventurae, 1924), 1, P1, In1, Tr1, Q3, C1, Ad 2 (n. 31), 50.

longest sections of the text cover God's infinity in relation to space and time. However, the prior sections are fundamental to outlining the Summa's position and will be the focus here, while the section on time will be treated further below.

In the first chapter of the tractate, the Summist inquires whether the divine essence is infinite as Greek fathers like Dionysius and Damascus affirm.[73] Initially, the Summa enumerates arguments against this view, starting with Aristotle's claim that terms like 'finite' and 'infinite' imply quantity, which the Summa denies can apply to God at least in a material sense.[74] Likewise, the divine essence cannot be infinite, because, according to Aristotle, this implies incompleteness, disorder, and potential or lack, which play no part in the divine.[75] Finally, the Summa observes that finitude can imply completeness, having an end, or being one distinct being instead of another. This would seem to suggest that the divine essence is finite, because it is complete in the supreme sense of the term.[76]

On the other side of the argument, the Summist notes that power and essence must be the same in God. As his power is infinite, his essence must be also.[77] Thus, in the resolution of the question, the Summist defends the claim that God is infinite according to substance and not finite, except if we understand finite to mean 'complete'.[78] According to the Summa, there are two ways of being complete, namely, from oneself or from another. That which is complete from itself is an end, whereas those things which are completed from another exist for the sake of the end, which is God.[79]

Here the Summist clearly if implicitly assumes Avicenna's distinction – to be discussed later in this book – between a being like God which is necessary or actual through itself, and beings which are actualized through another, namely, God himself.[80] As the one who bestows the perfection of existence on all beings that

---

[73] *SH* 1, P1, In1, Tr2, Q1, C1, Solutio, 56.
[74] *SH* 1, P1, In1, Tr2, Q1, C1, 54, 1: 'Finitum et infinitum congruunt quantitate.'
[75] *SH* 1, P1, In1, Tr2, Q1, C1, 54, 4.
[76] *SH* 1, P1, In1, Tr2, Q1, C1, 54, 2: 'Item, finitum et completum idem; sed divina essentia est completissima; ergo est finitissima.'
[77] *SH* 1, P1, In1, Tr2, Q1, C1, Contra a, 55: 'Idem est in Deo potentia et essentia; sed potentia eius est infinita; ergo et eius essentia. Et confirmatio istius rationis est: quoniam in summe simplici non differunt potentia et essentia.'
[78] *SH* 1, P1, In1, Tr2, Q1, C1, Solutio, 56: 'Proprie ergo est dicendum ipsum esse infinitum secundum substantiam et non finitum, nisi dicatur finitum "completum".'
[79] *SH* 1, P1, In1, Tr2, Q1, C1, Ad objecta 2, 57.
[80] Avicenna, *Metaphysics*, in *Avicenna Latinus: Liber de Philosophia Prima sive Scientia Divina*, vol. 1, ed. Simone van Riet (Leiden: Brill, 1977), 1.6, 44; trans. Michael E. Marmura, *The Metaphysics of the Healing* (Provo: Brigham Young University Press, 2005), 30: 'Impossibile est ut aliquid idem sit necesse esse per se et necesse esse per aliud: si enim eius esse esset per aliud, tunc impossibile

exist, the Summa concludes that God is infinite in two ways, namely, because he does not have an end, but is the being that 'finishes' or completes all things. Likewise, God is infinite because he is present in all finite things, while remaining separate from or outside of them. As the Summist clarifies, this infinity is not quantitative in a material but rather in a virtual sense, insofar as God is in all things by his essence and power, and thus by his presence.

In affirming this, the Summa signals conclusively its divergence from Aristotle's view that infinity 'exists through a process of one thing coming into being after another.'[81] So construed, infinity is defined in a negative sense as that to which something can always be added, which thereby denotes potential, imperfection and even chaos.[82] While Aristotle thus denies that there is an actual infinity, Avicenna affirmed that the infinite can in fact be traversed, at least given an infinite amount of time.[83] For there are potencies that can always be actualized and in turn render further potencies real or necessary. This positive idea of infinity clearly better anticipates the Summa's account, which conceives God as the one who realizes all actual finite beings. Although such an account might seem to suggest that God is merely the sum total of all finite beings, the Summa is clear that God transcends his creatures by virtue of serving as their cause: he does not belong to the genus of creatures but remains a fundamentally different kind of being.[84]

---

esset illud inveniri sine illo alio, impossibile igitur esset inveniri necesse esse per se; si enim esset necessarium per se, iam haberet esse, et illud aliud nihil ageret ad illud esse necessarium; quicquid enim est ad cuius esse agit aliud, eius esse non est necessarium in se.' 'It is impossible for a thing to be [both] a necessary existent in itself and a necessary existent though another. [This is] because, if its existence is rendered necessary through another, it cannot exist without the other. But [if anything] whatsoever cannot exist without another, its existence [as] necessary in itself is impossible.'

81 Sorabji, *Time, Eternity and the Continuum*, 211, citing Aristotle's *Physics* 3.6–7.
82 See Aristotle, *Physics*, 3.6 and Sorabji, *Time, Eternity and the Continuum*, 210.
83 Aristotle, *Physics*, 3.4–5. Jon McGinnis, 'Avicennan Infinity: A Select History of the Infinite through Avicenna,' *Documenti e Studi sulla tradizione filosofica medievale* 21 (2010), 212, citing Avicenna, *The Physics of Healing: A Parallel English-Arabic Text*, trans. Jon McGinnis (Provo: Brigham Young University Press, 2009), 3.4, 281–301. See Avicenna, *Physics*, trans. McGinnis, 3.9.2, 337–38.
84 See Schumacher, 'The Early Franciscan Doctrine of Divine Immensity,' 278–94. Côté, *L'infinité divine*. Schumacher, 'The Divine Nature,' 183–207.

The Divine Nature: Eternal or Everlasting?

The transition in thinking about the doctrine of God that I have traced above, according to which the concept of divine infinity gradually replaced divine simplicity as the primary, if not the only, feature of the divine nature, had direct ramifications for the way that God's eternity was conceived. As I will demonstrate below, proponents of simplicity like Augustine, Boethius, Anselm, and their scholastic followers, such as Peter Lombard, Alan of Lille, and even Alexander of Hales himself, generally speak of God as timelessly eternal. Accordingly, they refuse to describe God's knowledge in temporal terms and affirm that he sees the past and future as present in his 'eternal now', rather like someone standing on a mountaintop is able to survey a vast landscape beneath them.

By contrast, the early Franciscan authors of the *Summa Halensis* speak of God as a being that is not subject to a beginning or an end or to change and is therefore everlasting. Although the Summa clearly invokes Richard of St Victor's theological understanding of God's eternity in doing so, I will also show in a section further below that the authors draw philosophical inspiration from the metaphysical views of Avicenna, including his account of time, in order to define God not only as infinite but also as infinite in duration, or everlasting. First, however, I outline the contours of the classical arguments for divine timelessness before examining the Summa's position on God's eternal nature.

Augustine

Augustine's key insights on the nature of time, which are accompanied by influential reflections on divine eternity, are explicated in *Confessions* book 11. There, he emphasizes the fleeting nature of time: the fact that the present lasts only an instant as it rapidly flies from the future into the past.[1] For this reason, the past and future do not really exist, and only the present is accessible to us immediately.[2] According to Augustine, this raises the question how time can be measured, and in answering this question, Augustine famously turns to the human mind which alone can fathom what no longer or does not yet exist in time, by virtue of its memory of the past or anticipation of the future.[3] According to Augus-

---

[1] Augustine, *Confessions*, 11.15.18, trans. Bourke, 344–46. See also *Confessions* 11.15.20, 346: The present 'flies so rapidly from future to past, that it cannot be extended by any delay.'
[2] Augustine, *Confessions*, 11.18.23, trans. Bourke, 348–49.
[3] *Confessions* 11.15.19; cf. *Confessions* 11.18.23–11.20.26.

tine, this attending or 'stretching' of the mind (*distentio animi*) to past and future is that by which 'we perceive intervals of times, and we compare them with themselves, and we say some are longer, others shorter.'[4]

In reflecting on these claims, some commentators have argued that Augustine sees time as a purely psychological matter, which exists only in the mind or soul.[5] This notion, that time exists only in the soul rather than in reality, was among the 219 theses that were famously listed in the famous Parisian condemnation of 1277, which was ostensibly directed against Averroes but also potentially targeted other thinkers like Aquinas.[6] Specifically, article 200 condemns the idea 'that the aevum and time are nothing in themselves but only in the apprehension.'[7]

Those scholars who worked in the wake of this condemnation were constrained to avoid suggesting that time is purely subjective. Some did so by distancing themselves from Augustine while others sought to show that he did not merely reduce time to a function of the mind.[8] Similarly, a number of modern interpreters have stressed that time for Augustine comes into being with creation as something created and therefore has an objective existence outside the mind.

---

4 *Confessions* 11.16.21.
5 Jon McGinnis offers a psychological reading of time in Augustine in 'Creation and Eternity in Medieval Philosophy,' in *A Companion to the Philosophy of Time*, ed. Adrian Bardon, Heather Dyke (Oxford: John Wiley & Sons, 2013), 78. Robert Jordan opposes this view in, 'Time and Contingency in Augustine,' *The Review of Metaphysics* 8:3 (1995), 403: 'I admit that the bulk of Augustine's evidence is draw from the examination of consciousness, but I also venture to say that he discusses what is given to that consciousness and that it can, therefore, qualify as objective evidence.' At page 400, he also discusses Augustine's view of time as the extension between past and future moments, quoting *Confessions* 11.26–27.
6 Kurt Flasch, *Was ist Zeit? Augustinus von Hippo. Das XI. Buch der Confessiones* (Frankfurt am Main: Klostermann, 2004), 183. See also Anneliese Maier, 'Die Subjektivierung der Zeit in der scholastischen Philosophie,' *Philosophia naturalis* 1 (1951), 361–96. According to Maier at page 365, medieval Franciscans tended to derive the extra-mental reality of time from the undisputable reality of the present moment, which connects the future to the past and thus establishes their reality. By contrast, the Dominicans were inclined to attribute a mode of being to the succession of time in its totality.
7 Heinrich Denifle, ed., *Chartularium Universitatis Parisiensis* I (Bruxelles, 1964; repr. Paris: Fratre Delalain, 1899), n. 473, 554: 'Quod evum et tempus nichil sunt in re, sed solum in apprehensione.'
8 See Flasch's discussion of the medieval debate in chapter 6 of *Was ist Zeit?*, 160–95. See also Udo Reinhold Jeck's extensive discussion of the medieval theories of time in, *Aristoteles contra Augustinum. Zur Frage nach dem Verhältnis von Zeit und Seele bei den antiken Aristoteleskommentatoren, im arabischen Aristotelismus und im 13. Jahrhundert* (Amsterdam: B.R. Grüner, 1994).

After all, time must exist in some sense precisely as the interval that the mind measures in order for it to be observed in the first place.[9]

The interval itself, Augustine elaborates, is something 'we measure from some beginning unto some end.'[10] Time therefore appears simply to be the space between those two temporal points, one which comes first and one which comes later, much as Aristotle had suggested in offering his 'static' account of time. Augustine also speaks of time intervals in terms of the motions of bodies, some of which can be measured as longer or shorter.[11] Like Aristotle, however, he denies emphatically that time equates to those motions. After all, motion can be fast or slow, but time cannot. Instead, he suggests that time is the 'number' of motion, which again is measured by the mind.[12]

Although Aristotle's theory of time and 'Augustine's temporally structured, distended soul are not simply identical concepts,' Zachhuber argues in light of the foregoing that 'there are important agreements between the two which deserve to be noted without occluding differences.'[13] As we have seen, both Aristotle and Augustine seem to uphold at least elements of a static theory of time in which time is construed as the distance between two temporal moments, one prior and one posterior. This view ultimately lends itself to the idea that God is timeless, not subject to time in any way, since he neither comes into being nor passes away but is immutable and unchanging. So conceived, God sees all things that are past and future as immediately present.[14]

As Augustine writes: 'everything past no longer exists, everything future does not yet exist, therefore nothing past and nothing future exists. But in God's sight there is nothing which does not exist. Therefore, in God's sight, [nothing exists]

---

9 See for example Simo Knuuttila, 'Time and Creation in Augustine,' in *The Cambridge Companion to Augustine*, ed. David V. Meconi, S. J. and Eleonore Stump (Cambridge: Cambridge University Press, 2014), 81–97, esp. 89, where Knuuttila discusses some similarities between Aristotle and Augustine's views of time.
10 *Confessions* 11.27.34.
11 *Confessions* 11.23.30.
12 *Confessions* 11.24.31; cf. 11.26.33: 'I measure the motion of a body by time.'
13 Johannes Zachhuber, *Time and the Soul from Aristotle to St Augustine* (Berlin: De Gruyter, 2022), 80.
14 Augustine, *Confessions*, 11.11.13, trans. Bourke, 340: 'In eternity nothing passes away, but the whole is present. Now, no part of time is wholly present. So, it may see that every part of the past is forced out by the future, and every part of the future follows upon the past, and every past and future moment is created and flows from That which is the everlasting Present?' cf. *Confessions*, 11.31.41, 365–66.

as past or future, but everything is now.'[15] According to Augustine, this explains how the creation of the world does not imply a new will to create and thus a change which would be unbefitting of God.[16]

Furthermore, the idea that all things are present to God makes a mockery of those who inquire what God was doing 'before' he created the world, since there was no time before God created time itself.[17] Notwithstanding the strengths of Augustine's theory, Craig has observed that it might seem to suggest that God does not really possess foreknowledge of future events, since these are always present to him in his eternal now.[18] In this connection, Craig highlights the following passage from Augustine's *Eighty-Three Different Questions*, which seems to deny divine foreknowledge.

> What then is foreknowledge, if not knowledge of the future? But what becoming is there in God, who transcends all time? If then God's knowledge possesses the things themselves, they are not for Him future, but present. It follows that one may not in this case speak of foreknowledge, but simply knowledge. But if things which will exist do not yet exist for Him anymore than for creatures in the temporal order, but He foresees them by His knowledge, then He apprehends them in two ways: on the one hand, via foreknowledge of future things and on the other via knowledge of present things. Therefore, something temporal would be added to God's knowledge, which is both utterly absurd and utterly false.[19]

Although Augustine might seem to question divine foreknowledge in this context, the fact that he defends it in so many others suggests that he is mainly concerned here with entertaining possible objections to his position.[20] Indeed, the matter of

---

15 William Lane Craig, *The Problem of Divine Foreknowledge and Future Contingents from Aristotle to Suarez* (Leiden: Brill, 1988), 75, citing Augustine, *Eighty-Three Different Questions*, trans. David L. Mosher, in *The Fathers of The Church*, vol. 70 (Washington, D.C.: The Catholic University of America Press, 2010), q. 17, 45.
16 *Confessions* 11.10.12.
17 *Confessions* 11.12.14 – 11.13.15 – 16.
18 Craig, *The Problem of Divine Foreknowledge*, 73.
19 Craig, *The Problem of Divine Foreknowledge*, 73, citing Augustine, *De diversis quaestionibus ad Simplicianum*, ed. Almut Mutzenbecher, Corpus Christianorum, Series Latina, vol. 44 (Turnhout: Brepols, 1970), 2.2.2.27–36: 'Quid est enim praescientia nisi scientia futurorum? Quid autem futurum est deo, qui omnia tempora supergreditur? Si enim scientia dei res ipsas habet, non sunt ei futurae sed praesentes; ac per hoc non iam praescientia sed tantum scientia dici potest. Si autem sicut in ordine temporalium creaturarum ita et apud eum nondum sunt quae futura sunt, sed ea praeuenit sciendo, bis ergo ea sentit, uno quidem modo secundum futurorum praescientiam, altero uero secundum praesentium scientiam. Aliquid ergo temporaliter accidit scientiae dei, quod absurdissimum atque falsissimum est.'
20 Augustine, *The City of God I–VII*, 5.9, trans. Demetrius B. Zema, Gerald G. Walsh, in *The Fathers of The Church*, vol. 8 (Washington, D.C.: The Catholic University of America Press, 1950), 258–59:

God's foreknowledge is also treated extensively in Augustine's *De libero arbitrio*, specifically in relation to the question of its compatibility with free will. Augustine's way of resolving the apparent tension in this case involves affirming that while God's foreknowledge anticipates our choices, it does not cause them.[21] Thus, the necessity with which God knows what will happen does not translate into necessitating that it comes about. As Augustine writes: 'although God foreknows our future wills, it does not follow from this that we do not will something by our will.'[22] In this fashion, Augustine affirms God's foreknowledge of our future choices, in virtue of his knowledge of his eternal now, without compromising freedom.

Boethius

In his *Consolation of Philosophy*, book five, Boethius likewise addresses the question how God's foreknowledge can be compatible with free will. He summarises the problem as follows: 'if God sees everything that will happen, and if he cannot be mistaken, then what he foresees must necessarily happen.'[23] As Boethius elaborates, 'how can God know in advance that these things will happen if they are uncertain?'[24] This would suggest either that God does not have certain knowledge or, if he does, that what he knows must necessarily happen, which would undermine free will. In resolving this conundrum, Boethius argues along Augustinian lines that future events which are foreseen by God nevertheless do not occur *because* they are foreseen.

The reason God can foresee future events without necessarily causing them is that he is eternal.[25] On Boethius' much-discussed definition, 'eternity is the whole, simultaneous, perfect possession of limitless life.'[26] Whereas temporal things prog-

---

'God knows all things before they happen; yet, we act by choice in all those things where we feel and know that we cannot act otherwise than willingly.'

21 Craig, *The Problem of Divine Foreknowledge*, 73
22 Augustine, *On the Free Choice of the Will*, 3.3.7.28, trans. Peter King (Cambridge: Cambridge University Press, 2010), 78.
23 Boethius, *The Consolation of Philosophy*, 5.3, trans. David R. Slavitt (Cambridge, MA: Harvard University Press, 2008), 152.
24 Boethius, *The Consolation of Philosophy*, 5.3, trans. Slavitt, 154.
25 See Craig, *The Problem of Divine Foreknowledge*, 91–98.
26 Boethius, *The Consolation of Philosophy*, 5.5, trans. Slavitt, 168; see the extensive discussion of Boethius in Eleonore Stump, Norman Kretzmann, 'Eternity,' *Journal of Philosophy* 78 (1981): 432–3. William Lane Craig criticizes the Stump/Kretzmann and Leftow approaches to interpreting Boethius on divine timelessness, arguing that there must be temporality in God and in his

ress in the present from the past into the future, so that 'there is nothing in time that can embrace the entirety of his existence...[God] is an eternal present and has an understanding of the entire flow of time.'[27] In the context of offering an account of God's 'eternal present', Richard Sorabji highlights that Boethius distinguishes the 'now' of eternity from the now of *sempiternity* and the now of time, which are constantly flowing where eternity stands still:

> For our now, as if running, creates time and sempiternity, whereas the divine now stays not moving, but standing still, and creates eternity. If you add to that name the word 'always' (semper) you will create the continual, untiring, and hence perpetual race of that which is now, namely, sempiternity.[28]

As Boethius summarizes concisely here, God in his eternity is not subject to movement in any kind, like the now of time which is constantly changing and the now of sempiternity which moves perpetually in the same way. For this very reason, he is able to know all things 'in the simplicity of a continual present, which embraces all the vistas of the future and the past, and he considers all this in the act of knowing as though all things were going on at once.'[29] According to Boethius, this means that what we 'think of as his foreknowledge is really knowledge of the instant, which is never-passing and never-coming-to-be.'[30] On this basis, Boethius reiterates that divine foreknowledge does not make the future inevitable, but simply confirms God's awareness outside time of what we have yet to discover within it: 'his divine prescience does not change the nature of things, but he sees them in his present time just as they will come to be in what we think of as the

---

knowledge of he is to be related to a temporal world, in 'The Tensed vs. Tenseless Theory of Time: A Watershed for the Conception of Divine Eternity,' in *Questions of Time and Tense*, ed. Robin Le Poidevin (Oxford: Oxford University Press, 1998).
27 Boethius, *The Consolation of Philosophy*, 5.5, trans. Slavitt, 169.
28 Boethius, *De Trinitate*, in *Theological Tractates, De Consolatione Philosophiae*, trans. Hugh Fraser Stewart, Edward Kennard Rand, S. Jim Tester (Cambridge, MA: Harvard University Press, 1973), 4, 21–22, as quoted by Sorabji in *Time, Creation and the Continuum*, 116.
29 Boethius, *De Trinitate*, in *Theological Tractates*, 4, 21–22: 'But the expression "God is ever" denotes a single present, summing up His continual presence in all the past, in all the present – however that term be used – and in all the future. Philosophers say that "ever" may be applied to the life of the heavens and other immortal bodies. But as applied to God it has a different meaning. He is ever, because "ever" is with Him a term of present time, and there is this great difference between "now", which is our present, and the divine present. Our present connotes changing time and sempiternity; God's present, abiding, unmoved, and immoveable, connotes eternity. Add semper to eternity and you get the constant, incessant and thereby perpetual course of our present time, that is to say, sempiternity.'
30 Boethius, *The Consolation of Philosophy*, 5.5, trans. Slavitt, 170–1.

future.'³¹ The necessity of his knowledge of future events does not in summary amount to the necessity of what is known, which remains contingent along with the freedom of the will.

Anselm of Canterbury

In his classic discussion of divine eternity in the *Monologion*, Anselm argues that God has no beginning or end, because he was not brought into existence by another but rather exists through himself.³² As such, Anselm states that God or the supreme being is eternal. As he writes: 'That it always has existed, always exists, and always will exist follows from its neither starting nor ceasing to exist.'³³ To illustrate his point, Anselm argues that if truth had a beginning or an end, then it would be true that truth did not exist before truth began. Moreover, it would be true that truth no longer exists after truth ends. But true things cannot exist without truth; thus, the supreme Truth, God, is eternal.³⁴

On this basis, Anselm raises the question if and how the eternal God can exist at all times, whether as a part or a whole.³⁵ According to Anselm, God cannot be located partially in any place, as this would imply that he is subject to division or composition. For this same reason, he cannot exist as a whole in individual or distinct times or in time as a whole, as his being would seemingly be multiplied in the first case, while the second would suggest that his 'time span is not simultaneously as a whole. Rather it is stretched out in parts through time.'³⁶ As an eternal being, Anselm stresses that God is always fully himself, and thus he cannot be divided according to past, present, and future times.

How, then, is God present in time? In answering this question, Anselm stresses the difference between God and creatures. The latter are both present to and contained by time, whereas the supreme being is merely present to all times, insofar as, 'by its presence, it sustains everything other than itself, preventing everything from falling into nothingness.'³⁷ Thus, Anselm concludes that God is 'present as a whole simultaneously to all places and times, and to each individual place

---

31 Boethius, *The Consolation of Philosophy*, 5.5, trans. Slavitt, 171.
32 Anselm, *Monologion*, 18, ed. Davies/Evans, 31.
33 Anselm, *Monologion*, 20, ed. Davies/Evans, 33.
34 Anselm, *Monologion*, 18, ed. Davies/Evans, 32.
35 Anselm, *Monologion*, 21, ed. Davies/Evans, 34.
36 Anselm, *Monologion*, 21, ed. Davies/Evans, 36.
37 Anselm, *Monologion*, 22, ed. Davies/Evans, 39.

and time,'[38] insofar as those times are all simultaneous or instantly present to himself.[39]

According to Anselm's reasoning, this is possible because eternity 'is nothing but simultaneous and perfect existence.'[40] Similar to Augustine and Boethius, consequently, Anselm contends that God has no past or future but only his eternal present 'which contains both all things that happen at the same time and place and that happen at different times and places.'[41] On this basis, Anselm concludes that God knows immutably or necessarily what will happen in time, which is itself mutable or contingent. This raises the question, which Anselm addresses especially robustly in his *De concordia*, as to how divine foreknowledge is compatible with free will, since 'what God foreknows shall necessarily come to be in the future, while the things brought about by free choice do not issue from any necessity.'[42]

In addressing this concern, Anselm echoes Augustine and Boethius in insisting that the necessity with which God knows what will happen 'neither compels nor prevents the future existence or nonexistence of anything.'[43] 'Therefore, when we say that what God foreknows is going to happen is necessarily going to happen, we are not asserting always that it is going to happen by necessity but simply that it is necessary that what is going to happen is going to happen.'[44]

As Anselm reasons, God cannot *not* know what is going to happen, even if he does not compel it to come about. The reason for this, as noted, is that God is eternal and consequently sees all things not as past or future but as present.[45] Thus, Anselm concludes that there is no contradiction in affirming that something which is mutable in time, and which could thus be otherwise, is immutable in eternity, in virtue of God's eternal knowledge 'which embraces all time and all that occurs at any point in time.'[46]

---

38 Anselm, *Monologion*, 22, ed. Davies/Evans, 38.
39 Anselm, *Monologion*, 21, ed. Davies/Evans, 36; cf. *Monologion*, 22, ed. Davies/Evans, 39: Put differently, the divine essence 'is in every place and time because it is absent from none. It is in no place or time because it has no place or time.'
40 Anselm, *Monologion*, 21, ed. Davies/Evans, 41.
41 Anselm, *De concordia*, in *Anselm of Canterbury: The Major Works*, ed. Brian Davies, Gillian R. Evans (Oxford: Oxford University Press, 2008), 5, 443; cf. *De concordia* 5, 442.
42 Anselm, *De concordia*, 1, ed, Davies/Evans, 435.
43 Anselm, *De concordia*, 2. ed. Davies/Evans, 437.
44 Anselm, *De concordia*, 3, ed. Davies/Evans, 439.
45 Anselm, *De concordia*, 5, ed. Davies/Evans, 442: 'For in eternity a thing has no past or future but only an (eternal) present.'
46 Anselm, *De concordia*, 5, ed. Davies/Evans, 444.

Alan of Lille

Alan of Lille concurs with his forebears that God cannot be quantified temporally. 'For time is the duration and motion of mutable things. But there is no mutability, no motion in God, for He, remaining stable, gives motion to all things. Therefore, it [time] is not predicated of God.'[47] As Alan elaborates, time began to exist with the world, but God has always existed. Thus, he is not properly said to be in time. In this regard, Alan claims to follow Boethius who affirmed that all things both past and future are present to God.[48] Thus, the only sense in which God can be said to be in time is similar to the sense in which he can be said to be in a place, namely, not because he is constrained by space or time but because spatio-temporal beings come to be related to him through his creative work.

In light of these conclusions consequently, Alan states that there is no difference in meaning between the terms 'knowing' and 'foreknowing' in God. 'The difference lies in their connotation. The term "foreknowing" or "prescience" connotes anticipation of time, which is not connoted by the term "knowing" or "knowledge." Therefore, whatever God foreknows, He knows, but not vice versa.'[49] Thus, God cannot cease to foreknow something which comes about from the point of view of time, because he always knows it as present. For this very reason, his foreknowledge is not the cause of future events, for to know that they will happen is not the same thing as to make them happen.

Peter Lombard

In his *Sentences*, Peter Lombard codified the standard list of questions about divine foreknowledge in relation to his eternity that were commonly considered by subsequent scholastic authors, although most of his questions were also previously addressed by Anselm in some form. These questions included whether God

---

[47] Alan of Lille, 'La Somme,' 161: 'Tempus enim est mora et motus mutabilium rerum. Sed nulla mutabilitas, nullus motus est in Deo; nam stabilis manens dat cuncta moveri. Ergo de Deo non predicatur.' This is a direct quote from Boethius' *Consolation of Philosophy*, 3.9. Thank you to Oleg Bychkov for pointing that out to me.
[48] Alan of Lille, 'La Somme,' 162: 'Id est Deus habet presentia tam ea que fuerunt et futura sunt sicut et ea que sunt.'
[49] Alan of Lille, 'La Somme,' 240: 'Temporis enim anticipatio consignificatur hoc termino presciens vel prescientia, que non consignificatur hoc termino sciens vel scientia. Unde quicquid prescit Deus scit, sed non e converso.'

necessarily possesses foreknowledge, and whether this foreknowledge is the cause of or is caused by things, and whether things can happen other than God foreknows them.[50] In response to the first question, Lombard points out that God's ability to foreknow is the same as his ability to know and his ability to exist, which would seem to suggest that he would not be God if he was not able to foreknow. To answer this objection, the Lombard stresses that foreknowledge is a property of future things, not of the essence of God. 'Just as Creator is said relative to the creature,' he reasons, 'so also foreknowledge or foreknower is said with reference to future things.'[51]

Lombard next addresses a further objection that God might be said not to have foreknowledge, if there had not been things to foreknow. In response to this, he notes that the 'fore' in this context refers to temporal things, not to God.[52] The knowledge of God itself, according to Lombard, is eternal, so 'even if there were no future things, yet there would be in God the same knowledge as there is now, nor would it be less than now, nor is it greater than it would be.'[53] On this basis, Lombard concludes that, 'from eternity, God knew eternity and all that was going to be, and he knew it immutably. He also knows past and future things no less well than present ones.'[54] 'For all things are said to be present to him, not only those which are, but also those which have been and those which will be.'[55]

A further question Lombard addresses is whether God's foreknowledge is the cause of things. At first glance, this seems to be the case, because if God foreknows something, then it must come to pass, as his knowledge is infallible.[56] In this instance, however, Lombard points out that God would be the cause of the evils which he foreknows, which is impossible.[57] As Lombard thus elaborates, there is a difference between God knowing what will happen and his causing it to happen. According to Lombard, his mere awareness of what will happen is not causal. Conversely, future things are not the cause of God's foreknowledge, because he does not depend on creatures in any way.[58]

---

50 Anselm, *De concordia*, 7, ed. Davies/Evans, 447: Is God's foreknowledge the cause of or caused by things?
51 Lombard, *Sententiae*, d. 35.7.4, 195.
52 Lombard, *Sententiae*, d. 35.7.6, 196.
53 Lombard, *Sententiae*, d. 35.8, 196.
54 Lombard, *Sententiae*, d. 35.8, 196.
55 Lombard, *Sententiae*, d. 35.9.2, 197.
56 Lombard, *Sententiae*, d. 38.1.3, 213.
57 Lombard, *Sententiae*, d. 38.1.5, 214.
58 Lombard, *Sententiae*, d. 38.1.6, 214.

The Lombard finally raises a question whether things can happen other than the way God foreknows them.⁵⁹ This is impossible in Lombard's view because nothing escapes God's knowledge. As Lombard summarises, 'God knows simultaneously and unchangeably all things that were, are and will be, both good and evil; he also foreknows all future things, both good and evil.'⁶⁰ The reason for this is that God is eternal and thus sees all things which are past or future from the human point of view as if they were happening in the present, or now.

Alexander of Hales

In his Gloss on Lombard's *Sentences*, which was written between 1221–7, before Alexander became a Franciscan friar in 1236, the author affirms the classic view that, 'God does not know past or future because his essence always exists.'⁶¹ This for Alexander is what it means to say that God is eternal, namely, that he is not measured by temporal categories like past, present, or future.⁶² On Alexander's account, God's eternity is closely linked to and follows from his simplicity in the sense that God's essence and existence are the same – he is fully 'all at once' the substance that he is.⁶³

Put differently, God does not possess existence as an accident, or a quality which can be or not be in a being. As Alexander notes, existence is an accident in creatures, because they are from nothing, and thus have the possibility of not being. When they do exist, moreover, it is due to a composition of an essence and existence, or the fact that God has bestowed the property of existence on an essence that pre-existed in his mind.⁶⁴ In God himself, however, there is no such

---

59 Lombard, *Sententiae*, d. 38.2.2, 216.
60 Lombard, *Sententiae*, d. 39.4.3, 220.
61 Alexander of Hales, *Glossa*, d. 8, 5, 100: 'Cum ergo essentia Dei semper sit, non novit praeteritum vel futurum.'
62 Alexander of Hales, *Glossa*, d. 8, 6, 100: 'Patet ergo per primam partem quod non convenit Deo esse mensuratum praesenti, praeterito vel futuro.'
63 Alexander of Hales, *Glossa*, d. 9, 6b, 115.
64 Alexander of Hales, *Glossa*, d. 8, 10, 102: 'Esse non est accidens Deo. Cum enim vult distinguere per hoc creaturam a Creatore, esse est accidens creaturae. Respondeo: unaquaeque creatura, in quantum est de nihilo, possibilis est non esse; sed accidens est 'quod potest esse et non esse'; secundum hunc ergo respectum est accidens. Alio modo sumitur ut compositio essentiae cum eo quod est, et sic creaturae non accidit in Deo non differt esse et quod est.'

composition, for God is not a being whose essence cannot exist; or as Alexander puts it, essence and existence are the same in God.[65]

Since his essence always exists, he has no beginning or end and is therefore eternal.[66] As such, there is no part or aspect of him which is 'before' or 'after' but everything is simultaneous or present in his 'eternal now'.[67] In this regard, Alexander acknowledges a possible objection that God might be regarded as mutable, insofar as he existed before the creation of the world and thus 'began to be' the Creator at the point of his creation. As Alexander observes, however, the creation does not come from the substance of God but from nothing; as such, it does not bring about a change in God but only in bringing about the reality of creation itself.[68]

Here, Alexander clarifies the meaning of Lombard's claim that 'as Creator is said relative to the creature, so also foreknowledge or foreknower is said with reference to future things.' On his account, the term 'Creator' is relative to the creature in that God would not be called 'Creator' if the creatures did not exist. In other words, 'Creator' signals the relation of the creature to God rather than the other way around. However, foreknowledge is not relative in this same way, because God possesses this knowledge even if what he knows does not yet exist. Furthermore, God's role as Creator is said in relation to time, but God is not described as a foreknowing being as a result of any temporal event like creation, even though foreknowledge pertains to the temporal.[69]

In treating the topic of future contingents, Alexander differentiates between human and divine knowledge. The former is necessary or actual in relation not only to the knower but also to what is known, because we can only know defini-

---

[65] Alexander mentions a number of other kinds of composition which can be found in creatures but not in God, namely, that of causes, insofar as creatures rely on God as cause to their effect; composition of accidents; composition of forms, like soul and body; and composition of essence and existence or quod and quo est. See *Glossa,* d. 8, 20b, 105: 'Item, quatuor sunt quaestiones: si est, quid est, quid insit, propter quid insit. Scientiae autem horum ordinatae sunt super haec composita: "propter quid" dicit compositionem causarum; quid insit, compositionem accidentium; quid sit, compositionem formarum; an sit, compositionem differentiarum, scilicet "quod est" et "quo est". Haec ergo est compositio prima.'

[66] Alexander of Hales, *Glossa,* d. 9, IIb, 116: 'Aeternitas est duratio non habens principium nec finem.'

[67] Alexander of Hales, *Glossa,* d. 9, 13, 120: 'Quod in aeternitate non est pars post partem, sed totum simul; et hoc vult dicere per modo et modo.'

[68] Alexander of Hales, *Glossa,* d. 9, 7, 118.

[69] Alexander of Hales, *Glossa,* d. 35, 8, 353: 'Unde dicendum quod non est simile in Creatore et praescientia, quoniam Creator ex tempore et ad temporale, sed praescientia dicitur ad temporale, sed non ex tempore.'

tively things that are, not what could be. However, God's knowledge is not necessary or actual in relation to what is known but to the knower. As Alexander writes, 'God's knowledge knows things immutably through their entirely mutable cause, whether these things are mutable or immutable, which is not possible for human [knowledge]. For human [knowledge] either knows mutable things through a mutable cause or knows them mutably.'[70] This raises the question whether God's knowledge is temporal. As Alexander admits, this would seem to be the case, since God's knowledge is the same as his foreknowledge, and foreknowledge pertains to the future, which is a temporal category.

According to Alexander, however, God's knowledge is not temporal, because even though foreknowledge has reference to the future, it is not predicated in terms of time but exists from eternity. So 'although foreknowledge is concerned with temporal things, it is not called temporal because it knows temporal things in a non-temporal manner.'[71] From this point, Alexander turns to the question whether God's knowledge is the cause of things. He denies that this is the case insofar as the necessity that is inherent in the thing itself is different from the necessity imposed by the foreknowledge of God.[72]

That is to say, God's foreknowledge only allows him necessarily to know what will happen – it does not cause the actual event to happen. This solution bears on the ultimate question whether divine foreknowledge is compatible with free will.[73] On one level, it might seem not to be, given that God knows necessarily, and the will's choices are contingent. Here, Alexander distinguishes between an absolute necessary and a necessity of order. The former is causal, and the latter simply precedes the act of the human will. God's foreknowledge is not therefore the cause of the will but simply precedes and thus anticipates its choices.

In affirming this, Alexander signals his allegiance to the fairly traditional way of construing divine eternity and God's knowledge as an 'eternal now' which we have found in the works of Augustine, Boethius, Anselm, and Lombard. However, the approach of Franciscans more generally with whom Alexander came to be associated when he joined the order late in his career eventually diverged signifi-

---

70 Alexander of Hales, *Glossa*, d. 38, 3, 389–90: 'Divina scientia per causam omnino mutabilem immutabiliter scit res, sive sint mutabiles sive immutabiles; quod non poterit humana. Nam humana aut per causam mutabilem scit res mutabiles aut mutabiliter scit eas.'
71 Alexander of Hales, *Glossa*, d. 38, 4, 390: 'Et licet praescientia, non tamen ex tempore dicitur, quoniam intemporaliter scit temporale.'
72 Alexander of Hales, *Glossa*, d. 38, 5, 390–1: 'Restat ergo quod scientia Dei non est causa necessaria rerum...et non in hoc est identitas, quod, sicut hic sumitur necessitas ab ipsa re posita, ita et scientia Dei sumit necessitatem ab ipsa re.'
73 Alexander of Hales, *Glossa*, d. 38, 11, 392.

cantly from this paradigm, as is evidenced by the *Summa Halensis'* tractate on divine eternity, which was overseen by Alexander but likely authored by John of La Rochelle. This is the *Summa* to which we now turn.

The *Summa Halensis*

In its treatise on the infinity of God in relation to duration or time, the *Summa Halensis* defines eternity as 'duration without beginning and without end and without change.'[74] This definition clearly harkens back to Richard of St Victor's novel account of God's eternity, which he described as a combination of the definition of what it means to be everlasting – without beginning and end – and eternal, or without change. Although the Summa does not explicitly name Richard in discussing eternity, consequently, it does follow him in affirming that eternity, so construed, only befits the divine nature.

Like Richard, moreover, the Summa observes that its definition of eternity overlaps with that of sempiternity or everlastingness (*sempiternitas*), which can refer to something that always exists at every point in time, thus possessing a beginning but not an end. While divine eternity exhibits a kind of sempiternity, consequently, the Summa stresses that entities that are sempiternal are not strictly speaking eternal like the divine.[75] To illustrate this point, the Summa gives examples of beings that are sempiternal. For instance, angels are sempiternal because they have no end, either from themselves or from another, but they have a beginning at their creation by God and thus depend upon an external cause for their existence.

Likewise, the duration of the punishment of the damned is sempiternal, because it does not have an end from itself or another but has a beginning. Although heavenly bodies such as the sun and moon are immutable in their substance and lack an end, moreover, they do possess a beginning and are sempiternal. Time itself exhibits another kind of sempiternity, in that it has no end of itself – though it does have one from God. Nevertheless, it is subject to constant change and succes-

---

74 *SH* 1, P1, IN1, Tr2, Q4, M1, C2, 86: 'Aeternitas dicitur proprie diuturnitas sine principio et sine fine et sine mutabilitate: et secundum hoc convenit aeternitas soli divinae naturae.'
75 Tiziana Suarez-Nani, 'On Divine Immensity and Infinity in Relation to Space and Time: The Crossroad of the *Summa Halensis*,' in *The Legacy of Early Franciscan Thought*, ed. Lydia Schumacher (Berlin: De Gruyter, 2021), 82 in 71–88. *SH* 1, P1, IN1, Tr2, Q4, M1, C1, A1, 85, Respondeo: 'Sempiternum namque esse videtur quod caret initio et fine; aeternum vero quod caret principio et fine et omni mutabilitate et, quamvis forsitan neutrum sine altero inveniatur, recte tamen inter nominum significationes distinguitur.'

sion which makes it unlike God and in that sense not strictly speaking sempiternal.

Although the aforementioned forms of sempiternity are clearly inferior to divine eternity, which is not subject to a beginning nor an end nor to change, the Summa argues that sempiternal beings are analogous to eternity. In this regard, the Summa echoes the words of Alexander of Hales in some of his disputed questions, which were written after he became a friar in 1236. On Alexander's account, the analogy holds in virtue of an order of priority and posteriority between God and sempiternal beings, which Avicenna had incidentally invoked to develop his own account of analogy.[76]

As the Summa argues accordingly, created things are sempiternal because God is eternal – they are eternal 'through him' rather than 'through themselves'. In other words, they have elements of eternity because he causes them to do so, for instance, lacking either an end or changeability, but not both of those elements. As the Summa reiterates, only God possesses eternity in the full sense of the term, because he alone is immutable, beginningless and endless being. In other words, he does not move into being from non-being through the creative work of another but always is what he is through himself.

Precisely because non-being plays no part in his being, he cannot come into existence or to an end and is not subject to change, which is just what is entailed in any move from non-being into being or being into non-being.[77] Thus, he is eternal because he is a Necessary Existent – an argument which we will see below also derives from Avicenna. As such a being, God is not only the cause of himself but also of all other things that actually or could possibly exist.

---

[76] *SH* 1, P1, IN1, Tr2, Q4, M1, C1, A2, Respondeo, 85: 'Relinquitur ergo quod non dicitur aequivoce; erit igitur communis aliqua ratio, et si non omni modo, tamen secundum prius et posterius accepta. [Solutio]: Quod concedendum est. Dicendum ergo quod aeternitas, dicta de Deo, de angelo, de poena aeterna et der tempore, dicitur analogice, scilicet secundum prius et posterius. Et in hac ratione, secundum quod aeternitas dicitur diuturnitas non habens per prius ergo dicitur de diuturnitate divina, quae est diuturnitas non habens finem nec principium nec mutabilitatem ex se nec ex alio.' See *Alexandri de Hales Quaestiones disputatae quae ad rerum universitatem pertinent*, ed. Jacek Mateusz Wierzbicki (Grottaferrata: Collegii S. Bonaventure, 2013), memb. 1, 67–72. Other than that, Alexander's definition of eternity at memb. 2, 76–83, focuses more on the Boethian definition and construing God's eternity, like God himself, as a fundamentally different kind of thing from time or the aevum, although he does elsewhere gesture towards the Summa's idea of eternity as 'without beginning or end or alteration'.

[77] *SH* 1, P1, IN1, Tr2, Q4, M1, C4, Respondeo 1, 89: 'Nihil habet de non esse in suo esse admixtum; et quia nihil habet de non esse in suo esse admixtum, non est vertibile in non esse et ideo non potest habere finem.'

On this basis, the Summa links the idea of him as a Necessary Existent not only to his eternity but even more to his infinity, namely, because he is the one who cognizes and actualizes any of the infinite possibilities that exist in his mind.[78] He can do this because his own nature is fully actualized and thus precludes all potentiality, or the ability to change in any way. Although the Summa thus denies God's variability, its author allows that God can be said to exist yesterday and tomorrow in a qualified sense: that 'God was' or 'will be'.[79] This does not mean that God is contained in the places or times where he is said to exist, the Summa writes, but only that he is present to them as the one who contains them. The Summa quotes Anselm to reinforce this point:

> According to Anselm, it [the divine essence] is in every place and time, for it is not absent from anything; but it is in nothing, for it does not possess any place or time, nor does it contain the distinctions of places or times within itself, such as here or there, or in any other place, or now or then, or at any time, since these pertain to circumscribed and mutable things. And yet, in a certain way, these things can be said of it because it is present to all circumscribed and mutable things as if it were circumscribed by the same places and subject to the changes of times.[80]

In assessing this quotation from Anselm, the Summa acknowledges that affirming the presence of God to all times might seem to suggest that he is multiplied in himself. However, the Summa denies this can be the case on the grounds that 'eternity is a real unity which is in no way divisible,' and which 'is referred to in the plural [only] according to its infinite power to contain all durable things.'[81] More specifically, eternity is multiplied not in itself but 'because of the diverse participations

---

78 See Suarez-Nani, 'On Divine Immensity,' 84. *SH* 1, P1, IN1, Tr2, Q4, M1, C3, 87, Respondeo: 'Illud enim summe perfectum est, cui non est possibilis aliqua additio et ubi non est aliqua pars possibilis respectu totius: et simplicitate ista solus Deus perfectus est, quia quidquid est in eo ipse est. Per primum ergo separator esse aeternitatis ab omni corruptibili; per secundum ab omni variabili; per tertium ab omni composito, sive sit compositum ex materia et forma sive ex eo "quod est" et "quo est" sive ex differentiis.'
79 *SH* 1, P1, IN1, Tr2, Q4, M2, C2, Respondeo, 91.
80 *SH* 1, P1, IN1, Tr2, Q4, M4, C1, Ad objecta 2, 111: 'Unde notat quod, secundum Anselmum (*Monologion* 22): "In omni loco et tempore est, quia nulli abest; in nullo vero est, quia nullum locum aut tempus [habet] nec in se recipit distinctiones locorum aut temporum, ut hic vel illic vel alicubi aut nunc aut tunc vel aliquando, quoniam haec circumscriptorum et mutabilium propria sunt; et tamen haec de ea quodammodo dici possunt, quoniam sic est praesens omnibus circumscriptis et mutabilibus acsi illa eisdem circumscribatur locis et mutetur temporibus".'
81 *SH* 1, P1, IN1, Tr2, Q4, M2, C3, Respondeo, 92: 'Aeternitas est unitas secundum rem nullo modo divisibilis; tamen pluraliter dicitur propter virtutem infinitam continendi omnia durabilia.'

of eternity on the part of the creature or because of the power is multiple in its effect.'[82]

Here the Summa draws a comparison to the way God is present in the world in local or spatial terms, through the manifestation of his divine ideas in creatures.[83] In discussing this topic, the author distinguished between the divine essence, which is singular and one, and the ways in which creatures reflect him as their cause, or their relations of signification to him, which are many.[84] In this way, the Summa pays tribute to the traditional view God is not subject to temporal division, recognizing the idea that eternity is like a single instant, in which past and future are immediately present to God.[85]

At the same time, however, the author advances the novel claim that time is somehow present to God, in virtue of his 'infinite power to contain all durable things' as their cause. These indeed are insights the Summa seems to glean from the later work of Alexander of Hales, who writes in his disputed questions on the subject that eternity virtually contains infinite days and thus all times even though it is one total and perfect whole.[86] Through such forms of reasoning, we witness the shift in thinking of God as timelessly eternal towards understanding God's eternity in terms of his everlasting nature, which is infinite in temporal duration, 'without beginning, without end, and without change.'

---

[82] *SH* 1, P1, IN1, Tr2, Q4, M2, C3, Ad objecta 1, 92: 'Ad illud ergo quod primo obicit dicendum quod aeternitates dicitur pluraliter, non quia ipsa aetenitas plurificetur in se, sed propter diversas participationes aeternitatis ex parte creaturae vel propter virtutem continendi multiplicem in effectu.'

[83] Lydia Schumacher, 'The Divine Ideas in the Early Franciscan School at Paris (c. 1220–50),' in *Theories of Divine Ideas: From the Church Fathers to the Early Franciscan Masters*, ed. Tommaso Manzon, Irene Zavattero (Rome: Aracne, 2023), 237–59.

[84] *SH* 1, P1, IN1, Tr2, Q4, M2, C3, Ad objecta 2, 92: 'Ad illud vero quod obicit de pluralitate idearum, intelligendum quod dicuntur plures ideae et una, et plures rationes et una ratio. Respiciendo enim ad principale significatum, quod est divina essentia, una est idea et ratio, et una dicitur; respiciendo vero ad connotatum respectum ad creaturam, una est idea et ratio, sed tamen pluraliter dicitur, non quia plura sit vel intelligatur in rectitudine, sed plurium vel ad plura in obliquitate.' Cross reference to Alexander of Hales, *Quaestiones disputatae*, memb. 4, 92–3.

[85] *SH* 1, P1, IN1, Tr2, Q4, M2, C2, Respondeo, 91: 'In summa vero essentia unum tantum percipitur, scilicet quia praesens est, non quia continetur. Unde si usus loquendi admitteret, convenientius videretur esse eum loco et tempore quam in loco et tempore…Cum vero dicitur ' fuisse' vel 'fore ' vel esse', intelligitur praesentia eius omni praeterito, omni futuro, omni praesenti.'

[86] Alexander of Hales, *Quaestiones disputatae*, memb. 3, 87–9.

Metaphysical Foundations in Avicenna and the *Summa Halensis*

Already a couple of cases have been mentioned in which the *Summa Halensis* draws inspiration from Avicenna to lay a new emphasis on divine everlastingness. In what follows, I will delve more into the Avicennian metaphysical assumptions that made this focus possible.[1] Recent research has begun to establish the extent to which the authors of the Summa and members of this generation of scholastics more generally were influenced by Avicenna, whose massive *Book of the Cure*, containing treatises on metaphysics, psychology, theology, logic, and physics, was translated from Arabic into Latin between 1152–66, well before all the major works of Aristotle were available in sound translations.[2]

As noted already, Avicenna's writings successfully integrated Aristotelian and Neo-Platonic elements – which at the time were not seen as incompatible – albeit in a highly original way. His work therefore appealed to Christian Neo-Platonic thinkers who presupposed the tradition of Augustine but nonetheless wished to show engagement with the newly available major works of Aristotle.[3] Since Etienne Gilson first coined the term 'Avicennized Augustinianism', many scholars have conflated Avicenna's influence in this period with Augustine's and have therefore described early Franciscan texts simply as 'Augustinian'. However, recent studies have illustrated the considerable discrepancies between Avicenna and Augustine, who was mainly used as an authority to justify the appropriation of Avicenna.[4] In many cases, early Franciscans even used pseudo-Augustinian

---

[1] The material in this section is partly reproduced from Lydia Schumacher, 'Divine Power and Possible Worlds in Early Franciscan Thought: A Case Study in Avicenna's Reception,' in *Religionsdialoge und Wissensordnungen*, ed. Alexander Fidora, Matthias Lutz-Bachmann. Tübingen: Mohr Siebeck, forthcoming.
[2] Bertolacci, 'On the Latin Reception of Avicenna's Metaphysics before Albertus Magnus: An Attempt at Periodization,' 197–223; see also Bertolacci's, 'Reading Aristotle with Avicenna: On the Reception of the *Philosophia Prima* in the *Summa Halensis*,' in *The Summa Halensis: Sources and Context*, ed. Lydia Schumacher (Berlin: De Gruyter, 2020), 135–54. Magdalena Bieniak, *The Body-Soul Problem at Paris ca. 1200–1250* (Leuven: Leuven University Press, 2010). Hasse, *Avicenna's De anima*. Lydia Schumacher, *Human Nature in Early Franciscan Thought: Philosophical Background and Theological Significance* (Cambridge: Cambridge University Press, 2023).
[3] Lydia Schumacher 'Christian Platonism in the Medieval West,' in *Christian Platonism: A History* (Cambridge: Cambridge University Press, 2020), 183–206.
[4] Lydia Schumacher 'Rethinking the Reception of Augustine in Early Franciscan Psychology (c. 1230–45)', *Cithara* 60:2 (May 2021), 3–16; see also Schumacher's 'The *De anima* Tradition in Early Franciscan Thought: A Case Study in Avicenna's Reception,' in *Mediaevalia* 38 (2019), 97–115.

writings for this purpose, even though they were known to be inauthentic at the time.[5]

Although the Avicennian sources of Franciscan thought have now been demonstrated extensively in the field of psychology or the theory of knowledge, much more work remains to be done on his reception in the field of metaphysics, where his influence was particularly important for theological questions. To contribute to this study, I outline below some of the key facets of Avicenna's metaphysics, which were adopted by the *Summa Halensis*, and which ultimately if in some cases only indirectly contributed to the development of its views on time and eternity.

First and foremost, these include Avicenna's modal metaphysical distinction between necessary and possible beings, his proof for a Necessary Existent or God, his univocal understanding of the relationship between God and creatures, and ultimately, as I will show in a final section, the theory of infinite possible worlds, which served as a basis for the Summa's views on divine infinity. This metaphysical background lays the foundation for the subsequent section, which will elaborate how Avicenna's metaphysics informed not only Avicenna's but also the Summa's account of time.

Avicenna's *Metaphysics*

Avicenna's metaphysics rests on a fundamental distinction between necessary and possible beings. On his account, possible beings do not actually exist but nevertheless are not impossible and can conceivably enter into existence and thus become necessary or actual, though they need not do so.[6] In affirming this, scholars have noted that 'Avicenna rejected Aristotle's temporal (or statistical) interpretation of modality, which identifies necessity with actualization always, possibility with actualization at least once, and impossibility with actualization never, and allowed instead for both singular and universal possibilities that are never actualized in extramental existence.'[7] For Aristotle, there is no such thing as a possibility that

---

5 See Schumacher, *Human Nature in Early Franciscan Thought*.
6 Avicenna, *Metaphysics*, 1.6.1, trans. Marmura, *The Metaphysics of the Healing*, 30: 'Among them there will be that which, when considered in itself, its existence would be not necessary. It is [moreover] clear that its existence would also not be impossible, since otherwise it would not enter existence. This thing is within the bound of possibility. There will also be among them that which, when considered in itself, its existence would be necessary.'
7 Jari Kaukua, 'Future Contingency and God's Knowledge of Particulars in Avicenna,' *British Journal for the History of Philosophy* (published online 2022), 2 in 1–21. See especially also Simo

has not been or will not be realized in time, because a possibility that is always prevented from being realized is an impossibility.[8]

By contrast, Avicenna defines possibilities much more broadly in terms of anything that can but need not ever exist. As Avicenna writes: the possible 'at one time is that which is not necessary, or [at another] is the presently non-existent whose existence at any supposed moment in the future is not impossible.'[9] According to Avicenna, a possible being can only become necessary 'through a cause and with respect to it. For, if it were not necessary, then with the existence of the cause and with respect to it, it would [still] be possible. It would then be possible for it to exist or not to exist, being specified with neither of the two states.'[10] When such a possible is made necessary through a cause, Avicenna elaborates:

> Then existence, as distinct from nonexistence, would have occurred to it. [Similarly,] if it ceases to exist, then nonexistence, as distinct from existence, would have occurred to it. Hence, in each of the two cases, what occurs to the thing must either occur through another or not. If [it occurs] through another, then [this] other is the cause. And if it did not exist through another, [then the nonexistence of the other is the cause of its nonexistence].[11]

In Avicenna's view, consequently, a possible being becomes necessary when it receives the property of existence from a being that is already necessary. In consequence, the previously possible being becomes necessary through the causality of that being, or 'through another', and thus becomes capable of serving in its own right as a cause with respect to other possible beings.[12] According to Avicenna, the chain of causes can proceed in this way *ad infinitum* into the future. Nevertheless, Avicenna stresses that it cannot infinitely regress into the past but must ultimately

---

Knuuttila, *Modalities in Medieval Philosophy* (London: Routledge, 2020) which includes extensive discussion of Aristotle's theory around pages 1–14.
8 See the important discussion of Aristotle's statistical model by Jaakko Hintikka, 'Necessity, Universality and Time in Aristotle,' *Ajatus* 20 (1957), 65–90.
9 Avicenna, *Metaphysics*, 1.5, trans. Marmura, 28.
10 Avicenna, *Metaphysics*, 1.6.6, trans. Marmura, 31.
11 Avicenna, *Metaphysics*, 1.6.4, trans. Marmura, 31.
12 Avicenna, *Metaphysics*, 1.6.3, trans. Marmura, 30: 'From this it is [also] clear that it is impossible for a thing to be [both] a necessary existent in itself and a necessary existent though another. [This is] because, if its existence is rendered necessary through another, it cannot exist without the other. But [if anything] whatsoever cannot exist without another, its existence [as] necessary in itself is impossible. For if it were necessary in itself, then it would have to come into existence, there being no influence on its existence by way of necessity from that which is other and which affects the existence of something else.'

terminate at a being that is not merely necessary 'through another' but rather is necessary 'in itself'.

This being which Avicenna calls the Necessary Existent differs from all other beings in that it has no cause for its existence other than itself. In this regard, Avicenna argues that the very definition of the Necessary Existent provides proof of its reality.[13] As Avicenna stresses, there cannot be two such Necessary Existents, because then one would have to derive from the other and would not therefore be a Necessary Existent.[14] So construed, the Necessary Existent stands completely outside the genus or category of natural beings, even though there is an 'agreed' or univocal relationship between cause and effect which allows the effects to demonstrate he nature of the cause in a limited way. As Avicenna writes:

> This existent is not a genus and is not predicated equally of what is beneath it. Yet it has a meaning agreed on with respect to priority and posteriority. The first thing to which it belongs is the quiddity, which is substance, and then to what comes after it. Since it [has] one meaning, in the manner to which we have alluded, accidental matters adhere to it that are proper to it.[15]

The analogy Avicenna employs here to explain the relationship of priority and posteriority that holds between cause and effect, or Being and beings, is that of a substance and an accident, where the substance exists in its own right, but the accident's existence is dependent that of the substance. In a similar fashion, Avicenna argues, beings exhibit qualities possessed by the Necessary Existent because they derive their being from the Necessary Existent: they are necessary 'through another' rather than through themselves.

Avicenna's Metaphysics in the *Summa Halensis*

In the context of treating a range of theological issues, the *Summa Halensis* presupposes the various aspects of Avicenna's modal metaphysics outlined above, although it rarely mentions Avicenna explicitly, even though it quotes him almost verbatim on numerous occasions. Throughout its discussion of the relationship be-

---

13 Avicenna, *Metaphysics*, 1.3. See Lydia Schumacher, 'The Proof for a Necessary Existent in the *Summa Halensis*,' in *The Summa Halensis: Doctrines and Debates*, ed. Lydia Schumacher (Berlin: De Gruyter, 2020), 59–72. SH 1, P1, In1, Tr1, Q1, C1–2, 40–45.
14 Avicenna, *Metaphysics*, 1.6.10, trans. Marmura, 32; cf. 1.6.2, trans. Marmura, 30: 'We thus say: That which in itself is a necessary existent has no cause, while that which in itself is a possible existent has a cause.'
15 Avicenna, *Metaphysics*, 1.5, trans. Marmura, 27.

tween God and creatures, for instance, the Summa invokes the Avicennian distinction between a being that exists or is necessary 'through another' or 'through itself.' We have seen this already in the context of the Summa's discussion of divine infinity, where the author distinguishes between beings that are complete through themselves or through another:

> Completion is said in two ways, from itself and from another. *Completum ex se* (completeness from itself) is identified with the end (i.e. God), because the end is that which completes (i.e. gives existence to) all things. *Completum ex alio* (completeness through another) is only accepted in those things which are for an end. Therefore, the end is completed not from another but from itself.[16]

This fundamental distinction between a being that exists through itself or another also grounds the Summa's argument for the existence of a Necessary Being. Nevertheless, the author attributes it to Anselm of Canterbury, as part of a strategy for 'justifying' the importation of Avicenna's theory into the broadly Augustinian Christian tradition.[17] In a section on 'the necessity of the divine being' which seems to draw the inspiration for its title from Avicenna, the Summist argues that beings which exhibit truth, goodness, and other qualities require a cause, which cannot regress infinitely but must ultimately terminate at a being that causes itself and all other beings, namely, God.

By considering such beings, which can only ever be possible in themselves, in terms of their source or cause, consequently, the Summa concludes that we can come to the realization that God necessarily exists – unless we wilfully refuse to do so. As the Summa further echoes Avicenna in affirming, only God exists through himself, because beings besides him have a beginning and end and can thus in principle be thought not to exist.[18] To demonstrate why, the Summa utilizes Avicenna's distinction between existence (being) and essence (thing), which are the same in God while they differ in creatures.[19]

For this very reason, creatures can be understood without reference to their actual existence, namely, as possible beings. By contrast, God cannot be thought of as non-existing, precisely because the definition of his being is to exist through

---

16 *SH* 1, Tr 2, Q1, C1, Ad objecta 2: 57: 'Ad secundum dicendum quod completum dicitur duobus modis, scilicet ex se et ex alio. Completum ex se dicitur finis, quia finis est complementum; completum vero ex alio accipitur solum in illis quae. sunt ad finem; finis ergo completur non ex alio, sed ex se.'
17 *SH* 1, P1, In1, Tr1, Q1, C1, I-V, 40–2.
18 *SH* 1, P1, In1, Tr1, Q1, C2, Ar2, Solutio, 44–5.
19 *SH* 1, P1, In2, Tr1, Q1, T1, C3, A1, Ad objecta 2: 'In Deo non differt "quod est" et "quo est".' cf. Alexander of Hales, *Glossa*, d. 8, 12, 102: 'Deo non differt esse et quod est.'

himself, or to exist necessarily, and so to be the one through whom other beings exist, insofar as they do so. According to Avicenna, the divine causality of creatures results in an 'agreed meaning' between the properties of beings and the divine Being, such as unity, goodness, and truth, which they exhibit finitely and infinitely, respectively. In a passage almost directly transposed from Avicenna's *Metaphysics*, the Summa likens this agreed meaning to the type of similarity that exists between a substance and an accident:[20]

> They agree in that they are both [a type of] being, which is predicated of them in terms of priority: substance as [a type of] being serves as a substrate to its accidents, and therefore 'being' is predicated in a primary sense of substance, which is 'being' essentially, and in a secondary sense of accidents, which are 'beings' [by virtue of being] in something else.[21]

Although the Summa claims on the basis of this passage to advocate an analogical understanding of the relationship between God and creatures, its author subtly but clearly re-defines analogy in terms of Avicenna's univocal theory of being, according to which the finite and infinite exhibit the same qualities in different degrees, one as cause and the other as effect. The reason the Summa still rejects the language of univocity is that the author believes this would require a like-for-like comparison between finite and finite or infinite and infinite beings, rather than the proportional one that exists between infinite and finite beings, which allows the latter to positively divulge part of but not the whole nature of the divine.

---

20 Avicenna, *Metaphysics*, 1.5, ed. Van Riet, vol. 1, 40; trans. Marmura, 27: 'Dicemus igitur nunc quod quamvis ens, sicut scis ti, non sit genus nec praedicatum aequaliter de his quae sub eo sunt, tamen est intentio in qua convenient secundum prius et posterius; primum autem est quiditati quae est in substantia, deinde ei quod est post ipsam. Postquam autem una intentio est ens secundum hoc quod assignavimus, sequuntur illud accidentlia quae ei sunt propria, sicut supra diximus. Et ideo eget aliqua scientia in qua tractetur de eo, sicut omni sanativo necessaria est aliqua scientia.' 'The existent (*ens*), as you have known, is not a genus and is not predicated equally of what is beneath it, yet it has a meaning agreed on with respect to priority and posteriority [i.e. cause and effect]. The first thing to which it belongs is the quiddity, which is substance, and then to what comes after it [i.e. an accident].'

21 Translation by Oleg Bychkov, *A Reader in Early Franciscan Theology: The Summa Halensis* (Fordham: Fordham University Press, 2022), 99–100. SH 1, Tr Int, Q2, M3, C2, Respondeo, 32: 1: 'Convenientia secundum analogiam: ut substantia et accidens convenient in ente, quia dicitur secundum prius et posterius de illis: quia ens substantia est principium accidentis, et ideo per prius dicitur ens de substantia, quae est ens per se; per posterius de accidente, quod est ens in alio. Dicendum ergo quod non est convenientia Dei et creaturae secundum univocationem, sed per analogiam: ut si dicatur bonum de Deo et de creatura, de Deo dicitur per naturam, de creatura per participationem. Similiter omne bonum de Deo et de creatura dicitur secundum analogiam.'

Although the Summa adopts these and other fundamental Avicennian metaphysical positions, it does revise the Islamic philosopher's views as needed according to its own theological commitments and priorities. For instance, Avicenna's Necessary Existent only brings logical possibilities into existence.[22] By contrast, his early Franciscan readers held that God can perform logical contradictions and may even transgress the purposes of his own justice or goodness.[23] While the Summists admitted that God does not perform such acts in virtue of his ordained power, that is, what he has actually willed to occur, they maintained that his absolute power allows for the possibility of doing so.[24]

This distinction between God's absolute and ordained power had a prior history in the scholastic tradition where it was frequently invoked to differentiate between what God does and what he could theoretically still do. However, the Franciscans were unique in combining this distinction with Avicenna's metaphysical conception of necessary and possible beings, which they in turn stretched in order to conceive of an imaginary metaphysical universe – identified with the mind of God – which God could but does not necessarily realise. This brings us to the notion of infinite possible worlds, which the *Summa Halensis* develops at the inspiration of Avicenna's metaphysics, and which in turn helped in the development of the Summa's understanding of divine infinity.

Possible Worlds

Although Avicenna himself does not speak explicitly of possible worlds in his writings, he hints at their existence not only in the modal metaphysics discussed above but also in his theory of providence. The latter has recently been the focus of a study by Jules Janssens, who cites the following important quotation from Avicenna's *Metaphysics:*

> Providence consists in the First's knowing in Himself [the mode] of existence of the order of the good, in His being, in Himself, a cause of goodness and perfection in terms of what is possible, and in His being satisfied [with the order of the good] in the manner that has been mentioned. He would thus intellectually apprehend the order of the good in the highest

---

22 Avicenna, *Physics*, 3.11 and *Metaphysics*, 4.2.
23 *SH* 1, P1, In1, Tr4, Q2, M2, Ch2, Ad objecta I.1, 220. Jules Janssens, 'What about Providence and the Best of All Possible Worlds? Avicenna and Leibniz,' in *Fate, Providence and Moral Responsibility in Ancient, Medieval and Early Modern Thought,* ed. Peter d'Hoine, Gerd Van Riel (Leuven: Leuven University Press, 2014), 442.
24 William J. Courtenay, *Capacity and Volition: A History of the Distinction of Absolute and Ordained Power* (Bergamo: Pierluigi Lubrina, 1990), 73.

possible manner, whereby what He intellectually apprehends in the highest possible way as an order and a good would overflow from Him in the manner, within the realm of possibility that is most complete in being conducive to order. This, then, is the meaning of providence.[25]

As Janssens observes, Avicenna implicitly employs the concept of possible worlds in this passage, when he describes God as capable in his perfection of seeing himself as the source of all things that are and could be and thus of discerning all the unrealised possibilities – or possible worlds – he could yet instantiate by his will. For Avicenna, these possibilities are ones God knows in virtue of his knowledge of universals.[26] Thus, God knows particulars in virtue of his universal knowledge of himself as their cause. As Marmura points out, this is also how God in Avicenna's understanding knows future contingent propositions, namely, in virtue of himself as cause.[27]

According to Avicenna, the quiddity or essence of a thing can exist either in an instantiated individual or in the universal form itself, not to mention in the human mind. This view therefore created an opportunity, not fully realised by Avicenna himself but seized by early Franciscans, who argued that God knows both individual finite beings as well as universals.[28] As suggested already, this novel Franciscan emphasis on God's knowledge of individuals was accompanied by another innovation, not incompatible with Avicenna's thinking, that God, as the source and knower of all finite beings – whether actual or possible – is himself an infinite being.[29]

In turn, the plurality and indeed infinity of possible finite beings, which God possesses as ideas in his mind, and which he can potentially cause to exist, served as a key metaphysical factor that led the Halensian author himself to raise the

---

25 As quoted by Janssens on page 442 from Avicenna, *Metaphysics*, 9.6, trans. Marmura, 339.
26 Avicenna, *Metaphysics*, 8.7, trans. Marmura, 291: 'He intellectually apprehends things all at once, without being rendered multiple by them in His substance, or their becoming conceived in their forms in the reality of His essence. Rather, their forms emanate from Him as intelligibles. He is more worthy to be an intellect than the forms that emanate from His intellectuality. Because He intellectually apprehends His essence, and that He is the principle of all things, He apprehends [by] His essence all things.'
27 See Michael E. Marmura, 'Divine Omniscience and Future Contingents in Alfarabi and Avicenna,' in *Divine Omniscience and Omnipotence in Medieval Philosophy*, ed. Tamar Rudavsky (Dordrecht: Reidel, 1985), 88–91. See also Avicenna, *Metaphysics*, 8.6 on God's knowledge of particulars in virtue of knowing universals.
28 *SH* 1, P1 In1, Tr5, S1 Q1, M3, C6, Contra, 256: 'Ergo ipse Deus aequaliter est artifex magnorum et parvorum; ergo in arte sua aequaliter cognoscit magna et parva. Item, quod potest cognoscere creatura, non potest Deus ignorare. Si ergo creatura potest cognoscere singularia, Deus non potest ignorare singularia.'
29 McGinnis, 'Avicennan Infinity,' 199–222; cf. Avicenna, *Physics*, trans. McGinnis, 3.10, 4.15.

question of 'infinite worlds', which are logically and potentially really possible alternatives to the world in which we presently live. These worlds are ones God could create through his absolute power but does not through his ordained. Although the idea of possible worlds has often been associated with early modern thinkers like Leibniz, the *Summa Halensis* seems to offer the first clear statement of it, aside from the gestures from Avicenna.[30] As the Summa writes:

> In God there is the possibility of [making] infinite worlds (*infinitos mundos*); therefore it is possible for infinite worlds to be created. For as prime matter is a primary passive potential, so in God there is a primary active potential. However prime matter, insofar as its own primary potential is concerned, is not determined to any form but is indifferent to all forms. Nevertheless, matter is understood with a certain disposition [to forms] and so it is determined to some form. Similarly, it is said of the active potential of God that it is an undetermined potential, which has [the ability to make] infinite worlds, and according to this there is a potential in cause [or in principle] to make infinite worlds, and it is a determined potential through a preordained disposition.[31]

According to the *Summa Halensis,* the divine ability to create infinite worlds is another reason why God himself must be described as infinite: 'as therefore the body would be called infinite which would fill the whole world and exceed it, if there were infinite worlds, so the divine essence should be called infinite.'[32] While finite beings produce everything that they can produce in one act, the Summa elaborates, God, as an infinite being, is able to go on creating worlds as he chooses, to infinity.[33]

Although Avicenna is not invoked explicitly in reaching this conclusion, the foregoing discussion highlights how much philosophical work his distinction between necessary and possible beings performs at the background of early Francis-

---

[30] As Hintikka notes in 'Necessity, Universality and Time in Aristotle,' 77–8, the separation of temporality and modality which were held together by Aristotle is made complete by Leibniz but anticipated already by Franciscans like Ockham.
[31] *SH* 1, P1, In1, Tr4, Q1, M1, C3, Ad objecta 4, 204: 'In Deo est possibilitas ad infinitos mundos, ergo possibile est infinitos mundos creari: dicendum quod sicut in prima materia est prima potentia passive, ita in Deo est prima potentia active; prima autem materia, quantum est de sua prima potentia, non est determinata ad aliquam formam, sed indifferens ad omnes; sed tamen intelligitur materia cum aliqua dispositione; et sic est determinata ad aliquam formam. Similiter dicendum de potentia Dei activa quia est potentia indeterminata, quae se habet ad infinitos mundos et secundum hoc est potentia in causa ad infinitos mundos, et est potentia determinata per dispositionem praeordinatam.'
[32] *SH* 1, P1, In1, Tr1, Q1, C1, Contra d, 55: 'Sicut ergo corpus diceretur infinitum quod totum mundum mundum repleret et ultra, si essent mundi infiniti, ita divina essentia debet dici infinita.' See also *SH* 1, P1, In1, Tr4, Q2, M2, C1, Ad objecta I.3, 219.
[33] *SH* 1, P1, In1, Tr4, Q2, M2, C1, I.1, 218.

can accounts of the infinity of God and his knowledge, which extends not only to all necessary or actual beings but also an infinite range of as yet unrealized possibilities. By the same token, Avicenna's modal metaphysics informed the Summa's ideas about God's eternal nature, in ways that are summarized below.

Avicenna and the *Summa Halensis* on Eternity

As noted previously, the Summa defines eternity as an infinite duration without beginning, end, or change.[34] So construed, eternity shares much in common with sempiternity, or everlastingness, which involves existing at every point in time or never not existing, even though some beings which are sempiternal, like angels, are not strictly speaking eternal because they have a beginning in time or they change. The Summa employs Avicenna's modal metaphysics to affirm that such beings are sempiternal because they have some element of eternity through God's causality rather than themselves.

Again, echoing Avicenna, the Summa appeals to the idea of God as a Necessary Existent who exists 'through himself' in defining his eternal nature as everlasting. As Suarez-Nani observes, this understanding of the divine excludes all potentiality and all lack, presenting God as a fully actualized being who is the cause of his own existence and that of all other beings.[35] While such ordinary beings are subject to coming-and-ceasing-to be, God does not move from non-being into being. This is precisely why he is not subject to change and has no beginning or end: why he is everlasting.

As an everlasting being, we have seen that God is infinite, not in the 'negative' Aristotelian sense of a being to which something can always be added, which is thus imperfect and even chaotic, but in the 'positive' Avicennian sense of being present at every time. According to the Summa, all times are contained in his eternity, not as parts of a whole, since eternity is not subject to composition, but insofar as the whole exceeds or is 'outside of' its parts, as that which existed before, with, and after time.[36]

---

[34] *SH* 1, P1, IN1, Tr2, Q4, M1, C2, 86: 'Aeternitas dicitur proprie diuturnitas sine principio et sine fine et sine mutabilitate: et secundum hoc convenit aeternitas soli divinae naturae.'
[35] Suarez-Nani, 'On Divine Immensity,' 84
[36] *SH* 1, P1, IN1, Tr2, Q4, M2, C1, Ad objecta 1, 90: 'Ad illud quod dicitur primo: "tempus est pars aeternitatis": dicendum quod per similitudinem dictum est. Non enim dicitur "pars aeternitatis" eo quod integretur aeternitas ex tempore sicut sua parte, sed istud dicitur ratione durationis aeternitatis excedentis tempus. Pars enim et totum dupliciter comparantur: uno modo est comparatio substantialis, quia totum componitur ex partibus: et hoc modo non est tempus pars

This is quite a different approach to defining God's relation to time than we found in the classical accounts of Augustine, Boethius, and Anselm. These thinkers argued that eternity is like a single instant, in which past, present, and future are immediately present to God. Thus, God knows temporal events in an atemporal or 'tenseless' way, according to what McTaggart has called a 'B-theory of time', which allows for knowledge of 'before' and 'after' but not for temporality as such.[37]

The Summists also refuse to ascribe any temporal categories such as past, present, and future directly to God, as if he were subject to McTaggart's A-series. Nevertheless, they affirm God's ability to know things as past, present, and future, at least when his knowledge refers to the beings he knows, of which he is the ultimate cause. As we will see in the next section, this way of thinking about God's eternity is reinforced by the Summa's account of time itself, which entails the constant dynamic or flow of the 'now' of the present moment from the future into the past. This way of thinking about time also presupposes Avicenna's modal metaphysics, and indeed Avicenna's own account of time, in which each temporal moment represents a possibility that is rendered actual or necessary as time progresses.

The actualization of these possibilities occurs on account of God as the Necessary Existent, who is the cause of his own existence and that of all other things. As such a being, God knows in himself as the cause all beings that actually exist as well as all possibilities that could be realized at any point in time. Interestingly, it was precisely this idea that proved pivotal to Avicenna's theory of the eternity of the world, which like many of Avicenna's ideas, had its origins in the Aristotelian tradition. Although this topic has been discussed extensively by other scholars and is not our focus here, it is worth treating it very briefly simply to see how it features Avicenna's modal metaphysics and to discover how the *Summa Halensis* responds to the issue as well.

Aristotle and Avicenna on the Eternity of the World

As is well known, the question of the world's eternity remained a considerable preoccupation for Latin scholastic thinkers, virtually all of whom rejected it on the grounds, among others, that nothing created by God can be co-extensive

---

aeternitatis; alio modo est comparatio habitudinalis, secundum quod excedit omne totum suam partem: hac igitur similitudine dicitur tempus 'pars aeternitatis', quia exceditur ab aeternitate, quia ante tempus est aeternitas et cum tempore et post tempus.'

37 McTaggart, 'The Unreality of Time,' *Mind* 17:4 (1908): 457–74.

with him.[38] For thinkers like Aristotle and Avicenna, the rationale for affirming the theory derived from the account of generation or 'coming to be' that Aristotle presents in his *Physics* 1.7.[39]

In this context, Aristotle shows that any change requires the material that undergoes change, the form that is assumed through the change, and the initial lack of that form.[40] Aristotle himself used these ideas in *Physics* 8 to posit the eternity of motion, which he links inextricably to time as the 'number of motion'. According to his argument, motion and thus time must be eternal, because time could not have come to be in the first place if there was nothing from which it came to be. On this basis, many of Aristotle's commentators further argued that not only time but also the world must be eternal.[41]

Avicenna presented a version of Aristotle's theory, which presupposes his unique modal metaphysics. On his understanding, the world must be eternal because its creator is a Necessary Existent and thus his effects must also be necessary. For Avicenna, the suggestion that God began to realize the possibility of the world at a certain point in time and thus 'became' a creator implies a change in the divine which is unbefitting of his nature. Furthermore, it raises problematic questions about why God did not create the world earlier than he did or what he was doing before creation. To avoid these, Avicenna asserts that God necessitates his effects eternally and the world is therefore eternal.[42] For Avicenna, consequently, God exists prior to the world only logically and ontologically but not temporally: God and the world are essentially co-existent.[43]

---

[38] Luca Bianchi, *L'errore di Aristotele: la polemica contro l'eternità del mondo nel XIII secolo* (Florence: La Nuova Italia, 1984); *L'inizio dei tempi: antichità e novità del mondo da Bonaventura a Newton* (Florence: Olschki, 1987).
[39] See Aristotle's account of the eternity of the world in *Physics* 8.1 and *Metaphysics* 7.7–8.
[40] See Jon McGinnis, 'The Eternity of the World: Proofs and Problems in Aristotle, Avicenna, and Aquinas,' *American Catholic Philosophical Quarterly* (2014), 3. See also McGinnis, 'Creation and Eternity in Medieval Philosophy,' 73–86.
[41] McGinnis, 'The Eternity of the World,' 3. See also the discussion of Aristotle in Richard Dales, *Medieval Discussions of the Eternity of the World* (Leiden: Brill, 1990), 39–43.
[42] Avicenna, *Metaphysics*, 9.1.2, trans. Marmura, 300. Syamsuddin Arif, 'Neither Created nor Destructible: Ibn Sīnā on the Eternity of the Universe,' *Al-Shajarah: ISTAC Journal of Islamic Thought and Civilization* 25:1 (2020) 91.
[43] Avicenna, *Metaphysics*, 9.1.17, trans. Marmura, 304. Jon McGinnis, *Avicenna* (Oxford: Oxford University Press, 2010), 183.

The *Summa Halensis* on The Eternity of the World

Like most Christian thinkers at the time, medieval Franciscans opposed the theory of the world's eternity. According to Richard Dales, however, they opposed it to varying degrees, with some earlier scholastic thinkers, supposedly including Alexander of Hales, offering more moderate reactions to the theory.[44] Admittedly, Alexander does state in his disputed questions that philosophers like Aristotle could not have affirmed the eternity of the world, because they only discussed natural events existing in time, whereas creation is a supernatural event brought about by a divine creator.

Thus, Alexander concludes that Aristotle only meant to argue that the world is co-extensive with the whole of time, not with divine eternity. As he writes: 'since motion is commensurate to the whole duration of time, which has a beginning but not an end by its nature (except by the will of the Creator), in this sense, it could be said that motion is eternal and everlasting. We do not believe that philosophers spoke of it otherwise.'[45]

Nevertheless, Alexander mounts an extensive critique of the notion of the world's eternity, which has recently been explored by Toth.[46] Although Alexander acknowledges that God had the power to create the world from eternity, because he himself is eternal, he argues that God willed eternally for it to exist, not from eternity but from the time that he actually brought it into being. His will does not change in this regard, for he always willed that it should exist from the moment he caused it to exist.[47] As Alexander therefore stresses, the world cannot possibly be eternal like God because it is created; as such, it is 'from another', namely, God, without being from his divine substance but from matter, having being after non-being.

Although the *Summa Halensis* does not seem to copy much from Alexander of Hales' questions on the world's eternity, it also advances a series of arguments

---

[44] Dales, *Medieval Discussions of the Eternity of the World*, 65–67. Herbert Alan Davidson, *Proofs for Eternity, Creation, and the Existence of God in Medieval Islamic and Jewish Philosophy* (Oxford: Oxford University Press, 1987).
[45] See Alexander of Hales, *Quaestiones disputatae*, 'Questio de duratione mundi,' memb. 5, 189: 'Sed loquendo de eterno temporis, cum motus commetiatur se toti durationi temporis que habet principium, sed non finem, quantum est de se, nisi de uoluntate Creatoris hoc modo posset dici motus semper esse et eternus, nec credimus philosophos alio modo fuisse locutos.'
[46] Zita Toth, 'Creation,' in *The Origins of Scholasticism: Philosophy and Theology in Paris 1150–1250*, ed. Lydia Schumacher (Cambridge: Cambridge University Press, 2025), 237–59.
[47] See Alexander of Hales, *Quaestiones disputatae*, 'Questio de duratione mundi,' memb. 2, 171–4.

against the theory, many of which were later furthered also by Bonaventure.[48] At the outset of the discussion, the Summa acknowledges the typical Aristotelian/Avicennian view that the creation of the world depends on some pre-existing material from which it was formed.[49] According to proponents of the world's eternity, we have seen that this material must exist eternally in God, otherwise creation would involve a change in him or a transition from potency to act which is unbefitting of the divine.[50]

In response to this line of thinking, the Summa observes that everything that exists must proceed either from the substance of God, like the persons of the Trinity, in which case it *is* God, or from something other than his substance, and thus, from nothing.[51] 'If it is from God out of nothing,' however, 'then it has existence after non-existence and thus necessarily has a beginning of its duration.'[52] On this basis, the Summa concludes the world cannot be equal to its divine cause in its duration.[53]

In this regard, the Summa elaborates that the notion of the world's eternity is incompatible with the theory, itself Avicennian in origin, that the creature cannot exist through itself but only through another, namely, God.[54] As noted above, to be from another means possessing being after non-being and thus having a beginning in duration. Likewise, it entails being of a different substance to God, and thus inevitably being created from nothing. According to the Summa, God in his om-

---

[48] Thanks to Gloria Frost for pointing to me the similarity between Alexander and Bonaventure's arguments against the world's eternity and also the differences with Aquinas, who rejects the idea that creation entails having existence after non-existence and affirms instead that it only means that the world is not made of pre-existing matter.
[49] SH 1, P1, IN1, Tr2, Q4, M2, C4, Contra 14, 95.
[50] SH 1, P1, IN1, Tr2, Q4, M2, C4, Contra 17, 95.
[51] SH 1, P1, IN1, Tr2, Q4, M2, C4, c, 93: C, 93: 'Item, omne quod est a principio: aut procedit a Deo in identitate substantiae, et tunc, cum ipsa substantia sit aeterna, res sic procedens erit Deo coaeterna, quemadmodum Filius procedit a Patre in identitate substantiae et Spiritus Sanctus a Filio et Patre; aut procedit a principio Deo in diversitate substantiae, quemadmodum mundus a Deo. Primo modo quod procedit est Deus; secundo modo non, sed aliud in substantia a Deo. Hoc ergo quod sic est a Deo: aut est a Deo de nihilo aut de aliquo.'
[52] SH 1, P1, IN1, Tr2, Q4, M2, C4, c, 93: C, 93: 'Si est a Deo de nihilo: ergo habet esse post non esse et ita necessario habet initium suae durationis.'
[53] SH 1, P1, IN1, Tr2, Q4, M2, C4, c, 93: d, 93: 'Item, impossibile est effectum aequari suae causae, a qua differt in substantia.'
[54] SH 1, P1, IN1, Tr2, Q4, M2, C4, Respondeo, 95: 'Mundum esse ab aeterno, sive sine principio, est impossibile, quia esse aeternum, sive esse sine principio durationis, repugnat et creaturae et intentioni creaturae, sive eius quod est esse a Deo in diversitate substantiae.'

nipotence does not require any substance from which to create the world, because he is the sole cause of this work.⁵⁵

For the Summa, consequently, the doctrine of creation *ex nihilo* negates the need to explain how the 'stuff' from which the world came into being, without bringing about a change in God.⁵⁶ This is because the doctrine of creation from nothing makes it possible to distinguish the divine act of creation from any other kind of change. As the Summa affirms, the creation of the world only constituted a change on the side of creation, which began to exist in relation to God, who always exists unchangeably. For creatures, this relation to God is invariably qualified by a temporal component, which will be discussed at greater length in the section below.

---

55 *SH* 1, P1, IN1, Tr2, Q4, M2, C4, Ad objecta 12, 98: 'Ex parte divinae potentiae patet mundi exordium et materiae; nam divina potentia est summa et ideo non indiget materia subiecta ad operandum aliquid: est igitur operans de nihilo, quia est tota causa sui operis, ut non requiratur aliqua possibilitas ex parte subiectae materiae; ideo mutation prima circa operationem divinam non habet ante se mutationem aliam.'
56 On this see also, Alexander of Hales, *Quaestiones disputatae,* memb. 2, 174–7.

Time in Avicenna and the Franciscan Tradition

Although the Summa does not quote Avicenna explicitly in treating the nature of time, let alone eternity, as it does in other contexts, we have seen that its author clearly presupposes Avicenna's modal metaphysics and utilizes it extensively. The discussion that follows below will further illustrate how Avicenna's metaphysics laid the foundation for his understanding of time and eternity. Through an examination of Avicenna's views on these matters, therefore, we can assess the role they played in the development of the Summa's positions on time and ultimately eternity, and furthermore, on the question of God's knowledge of future contingents. Similarly, we can see how Franciscans working in the wake of the Summa developed their views on time in order to reach some of the more elaborate or even extreme conclusions about God's knowledge of the future which further reinforce the idea that he is essentially everlasting. To that end, however, we must first grasp briefly how Avicenna moves beyond the Aristotelian view of time which was otherwise dominant in the Middle Ages.

Aristotle on Time

Aristotle discusses time in his *Physics* 4.10–14.[1] He begins in 4.10 by considering various 'paradoxes of time'. One of these which proved particularly vexing for subsequent philosophers concerns whether the 'now' or the present moment remains the same or always changes. While there is always a 'now' at every moment in time, Aristotle concludes that the 'now' differs with each passing moment. In his preliminary remarks, Aristotle also evaluates some hypotheses about what time is which he however rejects.

For instance, he acknowledges that some say that time is the same as motion or change, but he denies that this is the case on the grounds that motion can be fast or slow, but time is only long or short. His well-known definition of time finally appears in *Physics* 4.11. This describes time as the interval between two different instants, or two 'nows', one of which comes before and one after. As Aristotle writes in this context:

> But time, too, we become acquainted with when we mark off change, marking it off by the before and after, and we say that time has passed when we get a perception of the before

---

[1] For a detailed interpretation of this passage, see Ursula Coope, *Time for Aristotle: Physics IV.10–14* (Oxford: Clarendon Press, 2005).

Open Access. © 2026 the author(s), published by De Gruyter. This work is licensed under the Creative Commons Attribution-NonCommercial-NoDerivatives 4.0 International License.
https://doi.org/10.1515/9783111705422-007

and after in change. We mark off change by taking them to be different things, and some other thing between them; for whenever we conceive of the limits as other than the middle, and the soul says that the nows are two, one before and one after, then it is and this it is that we say time is.[2]

The analogy Aristotle offers to explain his understanding of time is taken from the notion of local motion or movement between e.g. point A to point B, which involves traversing the distance between them.[3] In evaluating this account of time, Jon McGinnis has noted that Aristotle offers what might be called a 'static' account, in which time is conceived as the measure of the distance between two temporal points, one prior and the other posterior, which are analogous to spatial locations.[4]

This analogy presupposes the notions of actuality and potentiality, that is, potentially being at point B when one is actually at point A, and actually being at point B once one has traversed the distance between A and B. Thus, it presupposes Aristotle's famous 'statistical' or 'temporal frequency' model mentioned previously, according to which any possibility cannot be merely hypothetical or conceptual as it was for Avicenna but must have been realized at some point in time – otherwise we would not know for sure that it is possible.

On the basis of his spatial illustration of time, Aristotle draws his famous conclusion that 'time is a number of change in respect of the before and after.'[5] So construed, time is intricately linked to the human perception of time, since it involves our awareness of the interval between two points, one before and after. This has led to no little controversy amongst scholars who have debated whether Aristotle thinks time can exist without the soul or if it is merely a mental construct.

While scholars like Coope argue that time is soul-dependent for Aristotle, others like Sorabji claim that it is not. In his work on the subject, Johannes Zachhuber forges a middle way between these two extremes, suggesting that time involves both elements for Aristotle, namely, a subjective and an objective one. While

---

2 Aristotle, *Physics Books III and IV*, trans. Edward Hussey (Oxford: Clarendon Press, 1983), 4.11 (*219a22*), 44.
3 Jon McGinnis, 'Time and Time Again: A Study of Aristotle and Ibn Sina's Temporal Theories' (PhD: University of Pennsylvania, 2000), 155.
4 McGinnis, 'Time and Time Again,' 132–3. This claim is somewhat controversial: Richard Sorabji for one contends that Aristotle is somewhat indifferent to the distinction between static and flowing time and argues that he invokes both kinds of language. See Sorabji, *Time, Creation and the Continuum*, 47–50.
5 Aristotle, *Physics*, trans. Hussey, 4.11 (219b1), 44.

time serves as the measure by which the mind perceives changes, in other words, 'time is ineluctably part of the changeable physical world'.[6]

Avicenna on Time

In his *Physics*, Avicenna develops his thinking about time with reference to Aristotle's account, while at the same time making significant advances beyond it. As we have seen, Aristotle had conceived of time in 'static' terms as the interval between two temporal moments, one of which comes before while the other comes after. By contrast, Avicenna construes time dynamically as the continuous movement or flow of the present moment from the future into the past.[7] While Aristotle had focussed mainly on discussing the nature of time, moreover, Avicenna starts with a proof for the existence of time. This is not entirely relevant to our discussion here, however, which primarily concerns the nature of time.[8]

In treating this topic, Avicenna affirms in a way reminiscent of Aristotle that 'time is the number of motion when it is differentiated into earlier and later parts.'[9] As he elaborates, 'being divisible into earlier and later parts is a necessary concomitant of motion,'[10] because this involves movement from one place to another. Thus, motion numbers the earlier and later parts, by virtue of differentiating one from the other in terms of which comes before and which comes after. In turn, as noted already, time numbers the motion which does this differentiating.

So construed, time presupposes motion or change, because there can be no passing away of what was before or arrival of what comes after without some kind of alteration.[11] Thus, time on Avicenna's understanding is that on account of which the possibility of change exists and that in which the possibility of change is realized or rendered actual.[12] Avicenna illustrates this point by noting that if x is earlier than y, then x possesses necessary existence simultaneous

---

6 Zachhuber, *Time and the Soul from Aristotle to St Augustine*, 20.
7 Jon McGinnis, 'The Topology of Time: An Analysis of Medieval Islamic Accounts of Discrete and Continuous Time,' *The Modern Schoolman* 81 (2003), 18. Avicenna, *Physics*, 2.11, trans. McGinnis, 235: 'So time turns out essentially to have a before and an after; and so that which turns out essentially to have a before and an after we call time.' On the definition of time as the 'flowing now', see Avicenna, *Physics*, 2.12, trans. McGinnis, 244.
8 On Avicenna's proof for the existence of time, see for example McGinnis, 'Time and Time Again,' 216–23.
9 Avicenna, *Physics*, 2.11, trans. McGinnis, 232, 3.
10 Avicenna, *Physics*, 2.11, trans. McGinnis, 232, 3.
11 Avicenna, *Physics*, 2.11, trans. McGinnis, 233, 4.
12 Avicenna, *Physics*, 2.11, trans. McGinnis, 233, 4.

with the non-existence, but possible existence, of y.[13] Likewise, y becomes necessary or real when x ceases to be the actual state of affairs and falls into non-existence, unless x and y are simultaneous, in which case they can both be actual at the same time. On the basis of this illustration, Avicenna concludes that time 'turns out essentially to have a before and after'[14] because it is the measure of the changes or motion whereby the 'before' gives way to the 'after'. As Avicenna summarizes his position:

> How could there be time without before and after, and how could there be before and after when one thing does not come to be after another? Certainly, before and after do not exist simultaneously; but rather, something that was before ceases inasmuch as it was before because something that is after inasmuch as it is after comes to be. So, if there is no variation or change inasmuch as something ceases or something comes to be – nothing being after (since there was no before) or nothing being before (since there is no after) – time will not exist. In other words, time exists only together with the existence of the renewal of some state, where that renewal must also be continuous, otherwise, again, there will be no time.[15]

As Avicenna argues here, the transition from before to after requires the possibility of a renewal whereby one moment leads to the next.[16] To explain how this occurs, Avicenna introduces his notion of the present instant or the 'now', which is subject to continuous renewal, insofar as the 'now' that was before gives way to the 'now' that comes after. As Avicenna writes: 'between the time's existing and not existing, there is a certain division that is nothing but the existence of the present instant.'[17] According to Avicenna, there are two ways to consider this instant. The first is as a kind of boundary between the future and the past, namely, as that which demarcates one instant which is prior from another that is later. We can consider the instant in this way if we 'freeze' the motion of time, so as to discern 'the instant that divides the two times,'[18] namely, past and future.

The second way of considering the instant is in relation to time in its natural state of motion. In this case, we must recognize that this 'state does not remain the same at some instant or other, but, rather, at every instant, there is a renewal of a new proximity and remoteness, both of which result from the motion.'[19] Understood in this way, time involves the continuous movement of the present instant of

---

13 Avicenna, *Physics*, 2.11, trans. McGinnis, 234, 5.
14 Avicenna, *Physics*, 2.11, trans. McGinnis, 235, 5.
15 Avicenna, *Physics*, 2.11, trans. McGinnis, 235–36.
16 Avicenna, *Physics*, 2.11, trans. McGinnis, 236, 6.
17 Avicenna, *Physics*, 2.12, trans. McGinnis, 239, 2.
18 Avicenna, *Physics*, 2.12, trans. McGinnis, 242, 4.
19 Avicenna, Physics, 2.12, trans. McGinnis, 242, 4

time, which therefore 'produces a certain continuum through its flow.'[20] As Avicenna succinctly summarizes: 'the now produces times time through its flow.'[21]

In further discussing this 'now that flows,'[22] Avicenna considers the Aristotelian paradox whether the now changes or stays the same. The question, as Kolbinger nicely describes it, is whether 'this now which spans the time continuum, remains the same throughout time, or does it ever become different? Formulated differently: is time to be understood as the flow of a single moment, or rather as the succession of an infinite number of different moments?'[23] As Kolbinger sums up: Is there one now moving through time, or is time the succession of many different nows that come one after another?

Here again, as McGinnis notes, the now can be considered either in terms of the motion of the flowing now or as the boundary between future and past.[24] In the first sense, the now is an enduring feature of time insofar as it is what is present at every single point in time. In the second sense, however, Avicenna states that the present instant cannot exist twice, 'just as it happens that what is borne along qua being borne along cannot exist twice but passes away when it is no longer being borne along.'[25] For Avicenna, in summary, what it is to be a 'now' remains the same across time, but what it is to be a specific 'now' at a particular point in time always differs. In other words, the now remains the same according to essence but differs in its mode of existence across time.

This difference is paramount to emphasize for Avicenna because time is fundamentally a dynamic reality, which entails the perpetual 'ceasing to be of what is prior and a coming to be of what is posterior.'[26] One interesting feature of this account of time which McGinnis has highlighted is the way it effectively reduces temporal elements to modal and thus non-temporal ones, insofar as the realisa-

---

20 Avicenna, Physics, 2.12, trans. McGinnis, 243, 5
21 Avicenna, Physics, 2.12, trans. McGinnis, 244, 6
22 Avicenna, Physics, 2.12, trans. McGinnis, 244, 6
23 Florian Kolbinger, Zeit und Ewigkeit. Philosophisch-theologische Beiträge Bonaventuras zum Diskurs des 13. Jahrhunderts um tempus und aevum (Berlin: De Gruyter, 2014), 231: 'Die Frage lautete: Bleibt dieses nunc, das das Zeitkontinuum aufspannt, die ganze Zeit über dasselbe, oder wird es je ein anderes? Anders formuliert: Ist Zeit zu verstehen als der Fluss eines einzigen Augenblicks oder vielmehr als successio unendlich vieler verschiedener Augenblicke? Oder noch einmal anders: Ist das nunc – nicht spezifisch, sondern real und numerisch – ein einziges, oder gibt es zahllose verschiedene nunc?'
24 McGinnis, 'Time and Time Again,' 284; cf. 285: 'Insofar as it is what is flowing, it would remain one and the same, just as the object that happens to be moving remains one and the same. On the other hand, insofar as it is flowing it can be differently characterized.'
25 Avicenna, Physics, trans. McGinnis, 2.12, 244.
26 McGinnis, 'Time and Time Again,' 239. Avicenna, Physics, 2.11, trans. McGinnis, 236.

tion of one possible moment entails the 'cessation of the immediately prior moment,'²⁷ except in the case of possibilities realised at the same time, which are simultaneous.²⁸ On this modal account of time, McGinnis elaborates, 'if something exists for all time, it is necessary; if it exists at some time, but not at another time, it is possible; and if it exists at no time ever, it is impossible.'²⁹

Avicenna's account of time bears heavily on how he understands the eternal nature of God, whom we have seen he describes as necessary and indeed the *only* necessary existent.³⁰ So construed, God exists through himself: he is not originated by another but is self-caused and thus he serves as the cause of all possibilities that ever become necessary or actual. On this basis, Avicenna affirms that God has no beginning or end.³¹ To say that God is eternal, consequently, is to affirm that he is not subject to the possibility for change – and thus to coming to be and passing away, which is inherent in temporal beings that only exist if their possibility is realized by a cause. On this basis, Wisnovsky observes that God's eternality for Avicenna is 'to be defined as impossibility of non-existence.'³² For Avicenna, this is another way of saying that God is a being of perpetual or everlasting existence. As Avicenna puts it in his own words:

> The thing existing together with time, but not in time, and so existing with the whole of uninterrupted time is the everlasting, and every one and the same uninterrupted existence is in the everlasting. I mean by uninterrupted that it exists the very same, just as it is, at every single moment continuously. So it is as if the everlasting is a comparison of the permanent to the impermanent, and the relation of this simultaneity to the everlasting is like the relation of that instant of time to time. The relation of some permanent things to others, and the simultaneity that belongs to them from this perspective, is a notion above the everlasting. It seems more worthy to be called eternity. So, eternity is a whole uninterrupted existence in

---

27 McGinnis, 'The Topology of Time,' 13.
28 Jon McGinnis, 'Time to Change: Time, Motion and Possibility in Ibn Sīnā,' in *Uluslararası İbn Sînâ Sempozyumu Bildiriler*, vol. 1, ed. Mehmet Mazak, Nevzat Özkaya (Istanbul: Istanbul Büyükşehır Belediyesi, 2008), 251–57.
29 Jon McGinnis, 'The Ultimate Why Question: Avicenna on Why God is Absolutely Necessary,' in *The Ultimate Why Question: Why is There Anything at All Rather Than Nothing Whatsoever?*, ed. John Wippel (Washington, D.C.: Catholic University Press, 2011), 69.
30 Robert Wisnovsky, 'One Aspect of the Avicennian Turn in Sunnī Theology,' *Arabic Sciences and Philosophy* 14 (2004), 65–100.
31 Wisnovsky, 'One Aspect of the Avicennian Turn,' 69: 'Since there is nothing – apart from the eternal – that is not originated, this ultimate originator must be eternal. This eternal, ultimate originator is God.'
32 Wisnovsky, 'One Aspect of the Avicennian Turn,' 82–83; cf. 87: 'Thus all that is subject to change will itself be caused and possible, whereas all that is necessary of existence in itself will be necessary of existence in every respect, and no type of change whatsoever will be attributable to it.'

the sense of the absolute negation of change without a comparison of one moment after another.[33]

As this passage confirms, Avicenna defines the eternal divine being as an everlasting one who is not subject to the process of coming or ceasing to be that is inherent in possible beings. 'Inasmuch as the Necessary Existent is outside the temporal order,' Wisnovsky elaborates, Avicenna also cites ways of being eternal which can only be affected by the Necessary Existent; beings that meet this description, presumably celestial intelligences or angels, are what Avicenna describes as 'eternal through another' rather than 'through itself'.[34] This is how we will recall that the *Summa Halensis* referred to beings that are sempiternal, namely, that enjoy infinite or endless duration from the point of their creation, such as angels or human souls, which have a beginning and are not therefore eternal or everlasting in the full sense of the term. In what follows, I will explore further the *Summa*'s apparent development of Avicenna's account of time, which fundamentally depicts time as a kind of motion or constant change which involves the continuous flow of the 'now'.

The *Summa Halensis* on Time

The *Summa Halensis*' reflections on time are mostly to be found in the context of its discussion of the aevum.[35] This is a concept that the *Summa* itself was one of the first to formulate explicitly to explain the duration of permanent substances like angels. According to the Summa, these beings possess elements of eternity in that they have no end and are not subject to succession. However, they are not

---

33 Avicenna, *Physics*, 2.13, trans. McGinnis, 256–57.
34 Wisnovsky, 'One Aspect of the Avicennian Turn,' 79–80.
35 For a detailed study of the origins and medieval development of the concept of aevum, see, Pasquale Porro, *Forme E Modelli Di Durata Nel Pensiero Medievale: L'Aevum, Il Tempo Discreto, La Categoria 'Quando'* (Leuven: Leuven University Press, 1996); on the *Summa Halensis* and the role it played in the development of the theory of aevum, see 91–97. As Porro notes, Augustine conceived of the duration of angels as different from God's eternity but did not have a term for this (83); Boethius used aevum as a synonym for *aeternitas* (84). Porro provides an overview of the development of the concept of aevum in antiquity and the Middle Ages in 'Angelic Measures: Aevum and Discrete Time,' in *The Medieval Concept of Time: Studies on the Scholastic Debate and its Reception in Early Modern Philosophy*, ed. Pasquale Porro (Leiden: Brill, 2001), 131–59. See also the discussion of the *Summa Halensis* on time in Jeck, *Aristoteles contra Augustinum*, 202–5.

strictly speaking eternal because they are created and thus have a beginning, like beings which exist in time.³⁶

Also similar to temporal beings, angels are able to grow in their understanding and affection for the divine. When they do so, the Summa writes that the corresponding changes they undergo are measured by time 'or something behaving in the manner of time.'³⁷ Nevertheless, the aevum measures the actual substance of angels as permanent beings that continuously exist after their creation.³⁸ According to the Summa, the aevum governs not only the substances of angels but also human souls, insofar as they exist perpetually after they come into being. This raises the question for the Summa whether there must be different aevums to measure angels and souls, since the latter come into being at different points in time.

In addressing this question, the Summa ultimately concludes that while beings measured by the aevum have many different starting points, just like beings measured by time, both time and the aevum are one by virtue of their divine, eternal cause.³⁹ Not surprisingly, the Summa develops such views on the aevum in conversation with the main Latin Christian authorities on the subject, above all, Augustine and Boethius, and while there are some references to Aristotle, Avicenna does not feature as an explicit source in the discussion of temporality. Nevertheless, the Summa's understanding of time seems clearly influenced by Avicenna's dynamic idea that time is the continuous flow or 'motion' of the 'now' or present instant from the future into the past. This becomes apparent in the Summa's discussion of the relationship between the aevum and time.

---

36 *SH* 1, P1, IN1, Tr2, Q4, M3, C4, Ar1, Ad objecta 305, 103: 'Potest tamen dici unum ab unitate conformitatis, quia omnia aeva, distincta secundum distinctionem aeviternorum, conformitatem habent in imitatione aeternitatis et temporis: aeternitatis, quantum ad infinitatem ex parte finis et carentiam prioris et posterioris; temporis, quantum ad habere principium.' Also cited by Porro, *Forme E Modelli Di Durata Nel Pensiero Medievale*, 184.
37 *SH* 1, P1, IN1, Tr2, Q4, M3, C4, Ar1, Ad objecta 2, 104: 'In quantum vero habet esse in mutatione et motu, mensura ipsius est tempus vel aliquid ad modum temporis se habens.' On this, see also Alexander of Hales, *Quaestiones disputatae*, memb. 5, art. 3, 103. Porro, *Forme E Modelli Di Durata Nel Pensiero Medievale*, 214.
38 See a further discussion of the sense in which angelic being is measured by the aevum while changes in angelic actions are measured by time at *SH* 1, P1, IN1, Tr2, Q4, M3, C4, Ar2, 106–8.
39 *SH* 1, P1, IN1, Tr2, Q4, M3, C2, Solutio, 102: 'Si ergo simili modo se habet tempus ad aeternitatem, erit tempus unum, non ab unitate temporalium, quae mensurantur tempore, sicut patet ex praedicta sententia Anselmi, in libro De Veritate, sed ab unitate causae, quae est influentia seu virtus durationis ab aeternitate, secundum quod res sunt in participatiorie aeternitatis; simili modo unitas aevi, in quo est primo et principaliter influential virtutis durationis ab aeternitate.'

In this context, the Summa distinguishes between three ways of talking about time:[40] firstly, time is called the 'now' in an improper sense, namely, insofar as it refers to the beginning of time, at creation. Secondly, time is referred to in an even less proper sense as the 'now' insofar as it numbers what comes before and what comes after. In this respect, the Summa echoes Avicenna's argument that the 'now' is the boundary between the past and the future. The Summa further follows Avicenna in affirming that thirdly and properly, time is 'the continuous extension by way of the present ('the now') from the past into the future.'[41] Or as the Summa states: 'it is the continuum according to the continuity of motion in terms of what comes before and what comes after and the middle, which is the end of the previous and the beginning of the future.'[42]

In describing these last two types of 'now', the *Summa* gestures towards the distinction between so-called 'continuous' or 'discrete' time which became an increasing focus of debate amongst Latin scholastic thinkers in the thirteenth century. As Porro describes them, 'the former is produced by the flux of the instant proper (the now of movement) and receives from it its continuity; the latter is conceived by the succession of (improper) instants,'[43] which correspond to every point in a change. Aristotle – and Dominicans like Aquinas – adhere more to a notion of discrete time, where time is a matter of counting distinct moments or 'nows' that follow one after another.

Although the Summa acknowledges that discrete moments exist in time, at least when this is considered in an 'improper' sense, we have seen that its account of time in the 'proper' sense focuses on the continuous nature of time which is the product of a single now that flows from one point in time to another. For the Summa, this flow would seemingly be broken if time was simply reduced to a series of discrete entities which represent points on the continuum which follow one after the other. As Porro notes, the analogy many Franciscans including the Halensian Summists invoked to explain their view was that of a line, which is continuous

---

40 The discussion of these three 'nows' is found in other medieval/Franciscan texts, as Richard C. Dales notes in 'Time and Eternity in the Thirteenth Century,' *Journal of the History of Ideas* 49:1 (Jan-Mar 1988), 27–45. For instance, he mentions Alexander of Hales (p. 31), who treats the matter in his *Quaestiones disputatae*, memb. 10, 142–97; and Matthew of Acquasparta (p. 29), citing *Fr. Matthaei ab Aquasparta, O.F.M., S.R.E. Cardinalis Quaestiones Disputatae De Productione Rerum et De Providentia*, ed. Gedeon Gal, O.F.M. (Quaracchi, Florentiae: Collegio S. Bonaventurae, 1956).
41 SH 1, P1, IN1, Tr2, Q4, M3, C4, Ar1, Respondeo, 105: 'Proprie vero tempus extensio continua secundum praesens a praeterito in futurum.'
42 SH 1, P1, IN1, Tr2, Q4, M3, C4, Ar1, Respondeo, 105: 'Tempus est continuum secundum continuitatem motus secundum prius et posterius et medium, quod est terminus praeteriti prioris et futuri posterioris.'
43 Porro, *Forme E Modelli Di Durata Nel Pensiero Medievale*, 282.

because it can be divided many times without ever arriving at a minimum element – such as an instant in time.[44] The moment a minimum element such as a point is introduced, the line is broken into two, which cannot be the case of time, which is a single unbroken continuum.[45]

The Summa's view of time as a continuous motion or flow of the now is further confirmed in its pursuit of the question whether all forms of duration, namely, eternity, the aevum, and time, are characterized by some 'now' or present moment.[46] In answering this question, the Summa reiterates that the present moment of time is the beginning of the future and the end of the past, which is not the case for the aevum or for eternity.[47] Furthermore, the present moment of time flows with motion; in fact, it is created together with motion or the beginning of the universe.[48] By contrast, the present moment for both the aevum and eternity stands and remains without temporal progression from one moment to another.[49] On this basis, the Summa concludes that the 'now' of time, of the aevum and of eternity are only the same nominally. However, if we think of the 'now' in relation to the motion of a substance, then they differ.

> For there is a 'now' that is multiplied in time, just like the succession of motion itself. In this way it has the character of an instant and is called an 'instant' because it cannot stand still and is multiplied in time, having the character of continuity, insofar as it is the end of the

---

44 *SH* 1, P1, IN1, Tr2, Q4, M3, C4, Ar2, 108.
45 Porro, *Forme E Modelli Di Durata Nel Pensiero Medievale*, 310: 'For a quantity to be defined as continuous,' Porro writes, 'it must be divisible to infinity, without it being possible to arrive at a prime and minimum element...Where however it is possible to identify a prime and indivisible element, then the quantity (or the change) is of a discrete nature.' As Porro elaborates, the distinction between discrete and continuous time became a matter of significant debate, not least between Franciscans and eventually Dominicans like Aquinas, especially in discussing the 'temporality' of angels. While Aquinas advocated discrete time, where each angelic operation corresponds to an instant, such that angels move from instant to instant (318, 354), Franciscans argued that angels cannot move in such a non-continuous manner but must pass through the intermediate points so that their motions are continuous (349). See also Richard Cross, 'Angelic Time and Motion: Bonaventure to Duns Scotus,' in *A Companion to Angels in Medieval Philosophy*, ed. Tobias Hoffmann (Leiden: Brill, 2012), 117–47.
46 *SH* 1, P1, IN1, Tr2, Q4, M3, C1, 1, 99: 'Omnis duratio, sive sit esse creati sive increati, reducitur ad aliquod "nunc" vel praesens. Si ergo non est ponere nisi "nunc" durationis temporalis et durationis aeternae, ergo non erit nisi duplex duratio: aeterna et temporalis; ergo non est nisi aut duratio quae est tempus, aut duratio quae est aetemitas.' See also Porro, *Forme E Modelli Di Durata Nel Pensiero Medievale*, 31–2.
47 *SH* 1, P1, IN1, Tr2, Q4, M3, C4, Ar3, a, 109.
48 *SH* 1, P1, IN1, Tr2, Q4, M3, C4, Ar1, Ad objecta 1, 106.
49 *SH* 1, P1, IN1, Tr2, Q4, M3, C4, Ar3, c, 109. See the discussion of the Summa's argument in this regard in Porro, *Forme E Modelli Di Durata Nel Pensiero Medievale*, 152–4.

past and the beginning of the future, and it has the character of division, insofar as it is understood only as the beginning as the end. There is also the present moment that is the same in time and is not multiplied except accidentally. For in the same way that the thing that is moved is one in motion and is carried in one motion, so the 'now' is one which flows and is carried along through time. Finally, there is the 'now' that does not flow, just as something that exists is understood as remaining.[50]

This last now is the now of aevum and eternity, while the previous two types of 'now' pertain to the now of time. In the first case, the now of time is understood in its proper sense as akin to motion, or that which 'flows from the past to the future.'[51] On this basis, the Summa differentiates time from aevum as follows: 'After eternity, there is a 'now' or present moment that remains, not succeeding or continuing. This would be the 'now' of aevum. There would also be a flowing 'now' that succeeds and continues, which would be the 'now' of time.'[52] While the now of time in the first sense always differs through its continuous flow, the 'now' construed in the second way always remains the same insofar as it flows through every moment of time and is therefore multiplied only accidentally, while essentially remaining one and the same 'now'.

As the Summa reiterates, this way of thinking about the 'now' is less proper precisely because time does not stand still to be considered as such but is defined by its constant flow or motion. Thus, the Summa states that 'there is motion in the "now" of time as in its measuring principle.'[53] This is not true for angels are God, who is in the present moment not properly but as accompanying it or as present together with the present moment in time. As the creator of both the aevum and time, the Summa states that 'God is in all times, past, present, and future, because

---

50 *SH* 1, P1, IN1, Tr2, Q4, M3, C4, Ar3, Respondeo, 109: 'Est enim "nunc" quod multiplicatur in tempore sicut ipsa successio motus: et hoc modo habet rationem instantis et dicitur instans, eo quod stare non potest, et multiplicatur in tempore, habens rationem continuantis, in quantum est terminus praeteritio et principium futuri, et rationem dividentis, in quantum accipitur ut principium tantum vel ut terminus tantum. Item, est "nunc" quod est idem in tempore nec multiplicatur nisi secundum accidens: quemadmodum enim quod movetur est unum in motu et fertur in motu unum, ita "nunc" unum quod fluit et fertur in tempore. Item, est "nunc" quod non fluit, quemadmodum id quod est, in quantum huiusmodi, intelligitur manens.'
51 *SH* 1, P1, IN1, Tr2, Q4, M3, C4, Ar1, Ad objecta 1, 106: 'Et est "nunc" temporis, quod est fluens a praeterito in futurum.'
52 *SH* 1, P1, IN1, Tr2, Q4, M3, C4, Ar2, Ad objecta 5, 108: 'Et secundum hoc ponunt quod post aetenitatem est "nunc" sive praesens manens, non succedens nec continuans: et secundum hoc est "nunc" aevi; et est "nunc" fluens, succedens et continuans: et hoc modo est "nunc" temporis.'
53 *SH* 1, P1, IN1, Tr2, Q4, M3, C4, Ar3, Respondeo, 109: 'In "nunc" temporis est motus sicut in mensurante, et ideo in illo proprie.'

he is present to all circumscribed and mutable things as if he were circumscribed by the same places and subject to the changes of times.'[54]

This does not mean that eternity is composed of the parts of time but only reinforces that it exceeds all time, as that which exists before, with, and after time.[55] On this basis, the Summa rejects the idea that time can be co-eternal with God, even if we follow Aristotle in positing the eternity of the world, which entails that time has no beginning or an end. The reason is that eternity is invariable, but time as we have seen consists 'in the succession and flow of the present from the past into the future.'[56] As the Summa writes in its explicit rejection of the notion that the world is eternal, which will be discussed further below:

> Time has a beginning and time has an end. But I say that time did not begin in time, but in the 'now', which is its only beginning; similarly, time will end in the 'now', which is only its end, just as the 'now' that is continuous, in which the essence of time is preserved, is like the end of the past and the beginning of the future. Therefore, it does not follow that there is time before time or time after time, but only the 'now'.[57]

As the flow of the ever-changing present moment, the Summa insists that time – far from capturing the eternity of God – cannot even encapsulate the whole of time itself, that is, the 'infinite quantity of future and past'. Since it is bound to

---

54 *SH* 1, P1, IN1, Tr2, Q4, M1, C1, Ad objecta 2, 111: 'Unde notat quod, secundum Anselmum (*Monologion* 22), "In omni loco et tempore est, quia nulli abest; in nullo vero est, quia nullum locum aut tempus [habet] nec in se recipit distinctiones locorum aut temporum, ut hic vel illic vel alicubi aut nunc aut tunc vel aliquando, quoniam haec circumscriptorum et mutabilium propria sunt; et tamen haec de ea quodammodo dici possunt, quoniam sic est praesens omnibus circumscriptis et mutabilibus acsi illa eisdem circuniscribatur locis et mutetur temporibus".'
55 *SH* 1, P1, IN1, Tr2, Q4, M2, C1, Ad objecta 1, 90: 'Ad illud quod dicitur primo: "tempus est pars aeternitatis": dicendum quod per similitudinem dictum est. Non enim dicitur "pars aeternitatis" eo quod integretur aeternitas ex tempore sicut sua parte, sed istud dicitur ratione durationis aeternitatis excedentis tempus. Pars enim et totum dupliciter comparantur: uno modo est comparatio substantialis, quia totum componitur ex partibus: et hoc modo non est tempus pars aeternitatis; alio modo est comparatio habitudinalis, secundum quod excedit omne totum suam partem: hac igitur similitudine dicitur tempus "pars aeternitatis", quia exceditur ab aeternitate, quia ante tempus est aeternitas et cum tempore et post tempus.'
56 *SH* 1, P1, IN1, Tr2, Q4, M2, C1, Ad objecta 3, 90: 'Temporis, cuius esse est in successione et fluxu praesentis ac de praeterito in futurum.'
57 *SH* 1, P1, IN1, Tr2, Q4, M2, C4, Ad objecta 15, 98–9: 'Tempus incepit et tempus deficiet. Sed dico quod non incepit in tempore, sed in "nunc" quod est tantum principium ipsius; similiter desinet in "nunc", quod tantum est finis ipsius, sicut "nunc" quod est continuans, in quo salvatur essentia temporis, est sicut finis praeteriti et initium futuri. Ex hoc ergo non sequitur quod sit tempus ante tempus vel tempus post tempus, sed solum "nunc".'

the present moment, it is always fleeting and moving forward on 'the infinite journey of time'.[58]

Later Franciscan Accounts of Time

As noted previously, the *Summa Halensis* represents the first major statement of distinctly Franciscan views on time, to say nothing of many other theological and philosophical issues. As Kolbinger shows, the Summa's account of time as the flow or motion of the 'now' was elaborated by Bonaventure (1217–74), who was by far the most influential 'second generation' Franciscan, who helped further to establish the Franciscans in the new university of Paris.[59] However, Franciscan thought on time arguably found its fullest expression in the work of later thinkers like Duns Scotus, Peter John Olivi, Vital du Four, Richard of Middleton, and finally William of Ockham, who drew the explicit conclusion that time is essentially a kind of motion and reject the idea that time can at all be composed of discrete entities like the 'now', which would disrupt the continuum of time.

In what follows, I will trace the development of these later Franciscan views on time in order to help clarify how it was understood within this tradition. This will make it easier to see in the next section why so many of the same Franciscans discussed here eventually chose to emphasize God's ability to know the past, present, and especially future as such, rather than simply affirming that he sees all times in his 'eternal now'. This understanding of God's eternity matched well with the notion of discrete time in which the 'now' moves from instant to instant, whereas the Franciscan conception of time as a continuous flow fit better with an understanding of God as an everlasting being to whom that flow scan somehow be related.

As the following will illustrate, many of these later Franciscan scholars were concerned to discuss not only the nature of time in relation to eternity but also to affirm the real or objective existence of time, that is, its existence outside the mind. This matter became a preoccupation as a result of the growing circulation of the commentaries on Aristotle by Averroes, who actually did affirm that time is 'nothing in reality but only in the apprehension.'[60] Where Aristotle merely discusses the relationship of the soul and time, Jeck notes that Averroes posits time's de-

---

58 *SH* 1, P1, IN1, Tr2, Q4, M2, C1, Ad objecta 3, 90.
59 As Kolbinger notes in, *Zeit und Ewigkeit*, 194, Bonaventure adopts a lot from the *Summa Halensis* account of time and eternity (rather than the other way around), and this is one reason why the present text focuses primarily on the account of the *Summa*.
60 Jeck, *Aristoteles contra Augustinum*, 177. Flasch, *Was ist Zeit?*, 183.

pendence on the soul.⁶¹ He does this largely by stressing that the task of 'counting nows' which Aristotle described as something that must necessarily be performed by the soul.⁶² Outside the mind, there is only movement, but no way to divide it into earlier and later stages – and thus no way to track time.⁶³

As Jeck notes, Averroes' view was condemned in the famous censure of 1277 in Paris, specifically in article 200 out of 219, which states 'that the aevum and time are nothing in themselves but only in the apprehension.'⁶⁴ In some cases, Averroes' position was also linked to Augustine, on the grounds that the Bishop suggests in book 11 of his *Confessions* that the present alone exists and is immediately accessible us.⁶⁵ By contrast, the past and future exist only in our memory and anticipation, respectively.⁶⁶ As noted in the previous discussion of Augustine, the Bishop does affirm the reality of time as God's creation.⁶⁷ However, the relative ambiguity of his statements on the matter did create a perceived need on the part of many of the Franciscans discussed below to show that the reality of time can be affirmed. Thus, it is to their views that we now turn.

John Duns Scotus

John Duns Scotus (c. 1265 – 1308) is well known as one of the most influential Franciscan figures, whose thinking set his order on a new trajectory that was followed by many scholars for centuries. In fact, the Scotist school became one of the dominant forces in the late medieval and early modern university, along with the schools associated with Thomism and to a lesser extent Ockham/nominalism.⁶⁸

---

61 Jeck, *Aristoteles contra Augustinum*, 130.
62 Jeck, *Aristoteles contra Augustinum*, 132.
63 Jeck, *Aristoteles contra Augustinum*, 150.
64 Denifle, ed. *Chartularium Universitatis Parisiensis* I, n. 473, 554: 'Quod evum et tempus nichil sunt in re, sed solum in apprehensione.'
65 Augustine, *Confessions*, 11.18.23.
66 Augustine, *Confessions*, 11.15.19; cf. *Confessions*, 11.18.23 – 11.20.26.
67 Jeck, *Aristoteles contra Augustinum*. Flasch, *Was ist Zeit?* Zachhuber, *Time and the Soul from Aristotle to St Augustine*, 80.
68 Maarten J.F.M. Hoenen, 'Scotus and the Scotist School: The Tradition of Scotist Thought in the Medieval and Early Modern Period,' in *John Duns Scotus (1265/6 – 1308): Renewal of Philosophy*, ed. Egbert P. Bos (Amsterdam: Rodopi, 1998), 197–210. Jacob Schmutz, 'L'héritage des subtils: cartographie du Scotisme de l'âge Classique,' *Les études philosophiques* 60 (2002), 51–81.

Scotus discusses time at three main points in his work.[69] The first is in his commentary on Aristotle's *Metaphysics*, where he inquires whether time is the quantity of movement.

Secondly, he discusses time in book 2, distinction 2 of his *Sentences* commentary (all three versions – the *Lectura*, *Ordinatio*, and *Reportatio*), in the context of exploring the duration of angels. Cross dates the *Metaphysics* questions before all of the *Sentences* commentaries on the grounds that Scotus presents a different view in the former than in the latter.[70] In specific, Scotus claims to follow Aristotle in the *Metaphysics* commentary in stating that the present instant is the same or immutable as concerns its essence or substance but differs in its mode of existence insofar as it moves through time.[71] As Scotus summarizes Aristotle: 'The instant is in a certain way an ever immutable thing and in a certain way mutable and multipliable.'[72] To illustrate this claim, he asks his readers to

> Imagine that there is a point in motion, which makes a line through its motion. That point is simple because it is immutable according to its essence, but it is mutable insofar as a line flows from it. I say it is similar with the now, because considered according to its essence, insofar as it is simple, it is immutable and at rest. Inasmuch as it causes time through its flow, however, it is mutable and variable in its being.[73]

As Cross notes, Scotus moves away from this view of a 'flowing now' in his *Sentences* commentaries.[74] While that may seem to suggest that he changed his view, Boulnois notes that the relevant passage of the questions on the *Metaphysics* is almost entirely copied from the *Sentences* commentary of William of La Mare,

---

69 Olivier Boulnois, 'Du temps cosmique à la durée ontologique? Duns Scot, le temps, l'aevum et l'éternité', in *The Medieval Concept of Time: Studies on the Scholastic Debate and its Reception in Early Modern Philosophy*, ed. Pasquale Porro (Leiden: Brill, 2001), 161–88.
70 Richard Cross, *The Physics of Duns Scotus: The Scientific Context of a Theological Vision* (Oxford: Oxford University Press, 1998), 245.
71 John Duns Scotus, *Quaestions Subtilissimae super libros metaphysicorum Aristotelis*, in *Opera Omnia*, vol. 7, ed. Luke Wadding (Paris: Vivès, 1891), 5.10, 267: 'Illud instans secundum quod respicit eius essentiam est immutabile, sed inquantum respicit ipsum ut mobile circa locum est flexibile.'
72 John Duns Scotus, *Quaestiones*, 5.10, 267: 'Instans, inquit, est quodammodo quasi idem nunquam transmutabile, et quodammodo transmutabile et multiplicabile.'
73 John Duns Scotus, *Quaestiones*, 5.10, 267: 'Imaginetur punctum moveri, et per suum motum facere lineam, ille autem punctus est sic simplex, quia immutabilis est secundum suam essentiam inquantum vero linea fluit ab ipso, mutabilis est; a simili dico de nunc, quia secundum suam essentiam consideratum, cum sit simplex immutabile est, et stat; inquantum vero per suum fluxum causat tempus, mutabile et variabile, est secundum esse.'
74 Cross, *The Physics of Duns Scotus*, 245.

whose ideas Scotus may have drawn on while working through his own.[75] Scotus' early text also resonates with the account of the *Summa Halensis,* which affirmed the existence of a 'now' that remains the same as it moves through time – much like an object in motion – varying only accidentally or in its mode of existence at different times.

In the *Ordinatio,* Scotus contests the tendency thus to interpret the 'now' according to its substance or essence, as he had done previously in the *Metaphysics* commentary.[76] On his account, the 'now' is that by which we know what is prior and posterior in time.[77] However, it is not possible to know what comes before and after when we consider the 'now' in its substance but only under the aspect of change. The same is true of the object in motion, which carries the 'now' through time. While the moveable object always remains the same according to its substance and can exist without motion, motion cannot exist without the moveable object. On this basis, Scotus concludes that the 'now' cannot exist without time. Thus, it cannot be considered according to its substance, since it is always proceeding from one point to another and thus changing in terms of what it is.

Scotus further defends this position by arguing that the 'now' construed according to substance would be a sort of indivisible entity. As Scotus observes, however, Aristotle states that an indivisible cannot change or move because it always remains what it is.[78] Thus, the now considered as an invisible substance is incompatible with the constant flow of time.[79] In this regard, Scotus further points out that one and the same indivisible contains things which are simultaneous, so if an instant is the same according to substance, and thus an indivisible, all times must be equally present and simultaneous, which is absurd.[80] On such grounds, Scotus concludes that:

> The philosopher does not understand that the now remains the same according to substance, because the opposite follows from his statements. However, whatever 'now' is con-

---

75 Boulnois, 'Du temps cosmique à la durée ontologique?,' 161.
76 John Duns Scotus, *Ordinatio, Liber Secundus I-3,* in *Opera omnia,* vol. 7, ed. Karl Balić (Civitas Vaticana: Typos Polyglottis Vaticanis: 1973), 2.2.1.2, 199.
77 John Duns Scotus, *Ordinatio,* 2.2.1.2, 199.
78 John Duns Scotus, *Ordinatio,* 2.2.1.2, 200: 'Probat enim Philosophus ex intentione VI Physicorum quod indivisibile non potest moveri, quia tunc motus eius componeretur ex indivisibilibus, quia prius pertransiret minus vel aequale sibi, quam maius; igitur tempus esset compositum ex indivisibilibus, quod est contra Philosophum.'
79 John Duns Scotus, *Ordinatio,* 2.2.1.2, 200: 'Praeterea, quomodo posset ipsum "nunc indivisible" fluere secundum diversa esse (quae necessario essent indivisibilia), quin totus fluxus eius componeretur ex indivisibilibus.'
80 John Duns Scotus, *Ordinatio,* 2.2.1.2, 201.

sidered according to itself is the same, and this is what it means to be 'the same according to substance'. However, when considered in relation to time past and future, it is distinct in its being because it is the end of the past and the beginning of the future.[81]

In this context, Scotus again compares the 'now' to the movable object, which remains the same in substance before it undergoes change but changes continuously as it goes through any motion.[82] In a similar fashion, Scotus asserts that 'the instant throughout all time is different according to substance,'[83] because it is always subject the transition of the future into the past. By affirming this, Cross observes that Scotus effectively reduces time to motion, first and foremost, the motion of the outermost heavenly sphere, whose movements govern the temporal measurement of motion in our sphere.[84]

That does not mean that Scotus simply equates time and motion, however. The two concepts differ in his view insofar as all the parts of a motion do not necessarily correspond precisely in number and measure to the parts of time.[85] Depending upon the force used to move an object, for instance, it can move twice as fast, even though there will be no more parts of that motion in the period of time it takes to move than if the object than if it had moved more slowly. In this way, Scotus addresses Aristotle's claim that time must differ from motion, because motion can be fast or slow while time cannot. While all time is a kind of motion, on his account, not all motion is time.

Peter John Olivi

The Franciscan Peter John Olivi (1248–98) is perhaps most well known for his radical views on Franciscan poverty, which drew condemnations from his order but

---

[81] John Duns Scotus, *Ordinatio*, 2.2.1.2, 203: 'Ad Philosophum dico quod non intendit "nunc" manere idem secundum substantiam sed oppositum sequitur ex dictis eius; sed quodcumque "unum nunc" consideratum secundum se, est idem, et hoc dicitur esse "idem secundum substantiam" consideratum autem in ordine ad tempus praeteritum et futurum, cum sit terminus praeteriti et initium futuri, dicitur 'distingui secundum esse.' See also Cross, *The Physics of Duns Scotus*, 246–7.
[82] John Duns Scotus, *Ordinatio*, 2.2.1.2, 203.
[83] John Duns Scotus, *Ordinatio*, 2.2.1.2, 204: 'Igitur instans in toto tempore vere est "aliud et aliud" secundum substantiam.'
[84] Cross, *The Physics of Duns Scotus*, 233–4.
[85] John Duns Scotus, *Ordinatio*, 2.2.1.2, resp. 205–6.

did not necessarily impede his influence.[86] In his quodlibetal questions, he addresses two key questions concerning the nature of time: whether it is the same as the 'flowing now' (*nunc fluens*) and whether it has any existence outside the mind or soul. As we have seen, this question was at the forefront of scholars' minds in the wake of the 1277 condemnation in Paris.[87] In addressing the first question, whether time is the same as the 'flowing now', Olivi acknowledges a number of different interpretations of the 'now'. One affirms that the now remains the same through all times in its essence, even though it differs according to the course of its flux. In this regard, Olivi observes that some scholars went so far as to say that time is nothing other than the 'now' or the present instant.[88] Others hold that the flux of time adds something to its essence, while others insist that there is no 'now' that actually exists except at the beginning and end of time, just as no point actually exists in a line except at its two extreme termini.

Olivi presents three arguments in favor of this last view.[89] The first is derived from motion, whose duration is the same as time and vice versa. As Olivi notes, the end of a motion cannot exist simultaneously with the motion itself, and so similarly, no 'now' of time can co-exist with the whole of time and all its parts. Just as the position of a moving object ceases to exist as it moves, so, too, Olivi argues does its duration cease in its very essence to exist; thus, the now is constantly corrupted.[90]

The second argument Olivi offers invokes the concept of the aevum. If the flowing now remains the same for all time, he reasons, then it is essentially a continuously enduring 'now', which is nothing other than the aevum. This however cannot be the case because time involves the continuous coming and going of its parts, by contrast to the aevum which permanently endures. The third argument Olivi presents concerns the relation of the 'now' to its flux. According to Olivi, the now cannot be the same as its flux, because the now always remains the same, just as a moving object remains the same throughout the whole of its motion, while the flow of time is subject to constant change.

---

[86] David Burr, *Olivi and Franciscan Poverty: The Origins of the 'Usus Pauper' Controversy* (Philadelphia: University of Pennsylvania Press, 1989).
[87] See Jeck's full discussion of Olivi in *Aristoteles contra Augustinum*, 399–425.
[88] Peter John Olivi, *Quodlibeta Quinque*, ed. Stephanus Defraia (Grottaferrata: Collegii S. Bonaventurae, 2002), 1, q. 2, 8–9.
[89] These arguments are discussed by Jeck in *Aristoteles contra Augustinum*, 410–11.
[90] Jeck summnarizes Olivi's position in, *Aristoteles contra Augustinum*, 409: 'The continuous flow of time shows that one part of time follows another without interruption. One section of time passes while the other section of the continuum comes to present existence.'

The next question Olivi addresses is whether time exists outside the soul. Averroes denied that it does, and Olivi seems to think Augustine did so as well when he affirmed that the present is all that exists, while the past and future are only in the mind's memory and anticipation respectively. In response to these ideas, Olivi observes that we can think of the existence of time in two ways. First, we can consider it as a whole in its entirety, and in that sense, Olivi concedes that time mainly exists in our understanding, because all the parts of time cannot exist at once except in our thinking. 'Secondly, however, we can think of time as something in which one part truly comes to be and exists after another, and as something in which one part passes away and another truly arrives; in this sense, time truly exists in things, outside of the apprehension of the soul.'[91] Olivi offers three proofs for the extra-mental existence of time.[92] The first concerns the relation of time to motion. According to Olivi:

> Whoever denies that motion exists in things outside the soul denies sense experience itself, for we undeniably sense and see many things moving and many motions occurring in them…However, motion cannot exist outside [of the mind] without its duration also existing outside with it and within it. But time is the same as the duration of motion; therefore, it follows that time truly exists outside [the mind], just as motion does.[93]

The second argument concerns the relation of time to its parts. If time were not in things outside the soul, Olivi reasons, then nothing could really pass away or come to be in the present, which again contradicts sense experience, in which we encounter the flow or succession of time. The third argument is that we perceive time according to the categories of past, present, and future, contra Augustine who suggests that the present alone exists. In replying to the objections to his position, Olivi first addresses Averroes' interpretation of Aristotle's claim that 'time is the number of motion according to before and after'.

Here, Olivi argues that the distinction between the parts of time cannot be actual in any continuum like time, but only potential, since the actual distinction ex-

---

[91] Peter John Olivi, *Quodlibeta* 1, q. 2, 12: 'Secundo modo secundum quod una eius pars uere fit et existit post alteram, et secundum quod una inde preterit, et alia uere aduenit; et sic uere est in rebus extra apprehensionem anime.'
[92] These are discussed by Jeck in *Aristoteles contra Augustinum*, 410–11.
[93] Peter John Olivi, *Quodlibeta* 1, q. 3, 12: 'Primo, scilicet ex respectu temporis ad motum. Qui enim negat motum esse in rebus extra animam, negat sensum; quia indubitabiliter sentimus et uidemus multas res moueri et multos motus in eis fieri…Sed motus non potest esse extra, quin eius duratio sit extra cum ipso et in ipso. Tempus autem est idem quod duratio motus. Ergo uere tempus est extra, sicut et motus.'

ists only in the soul, which differentiates the parts of motion and time as prior or posterior, while time itself remains continuous. On this account, time is not the number of motion, because number concerns discrete entities or 'nows', and precisely because it is a single continuum, time is not a matter of 'counting' nows or discrete moments that come one after another.

Relatedly, Olivi responds to Augustine's idea that the present alone is real, by observing that 'one part of time comes to be as another passes away, so that no part of it exists as a whole at the same time.'[94] In this way, Olivi contests the idea that time exits at any single instant, on the grounds that it is in a continuous and flowing process of becoming (*in continuo et successiuo fieri*), such that the present moment always represents a part but not the whole of time.[95] In affirming this, Jeck notes that Olivi rejects the idea that the 'now' or the present instant can somehow located as a particular point other than at the beginning and end of time.[96] If it were otherwise, Olivi argues, then time would be divided into two separate continuums. Thus, Olivi concludes that the 'now' exists only in our imagination, which tries to pinpoint something that is actually always fleeting and constantly in motion.

Vital du Four

Like many of his contemporaries working after 1277, the Franciscan Vital du Four (1260–1327) approaches the topic of time from the perspective of the question whether it exists outside the soul.[97] In this regard, he notes that there are three important aspects of time to consider. The first is that time is co-extensive with motion, as the measure of its duration. Second, time is number, not a 'numbering number' (*numerus numerans*) but that which is numbered (*numeratus*), namely, the motion of an object.[98] Thirdly, time is taken as the measure of motion, and since a measure must certify what is measured, it exists in the soul by way of certification and cognition.

In response to Aristotle, other philosophers, and Augustine, Vital contests the idea that time is continuous simply because past and future are connected

---

[94] Peter John Olivi, *Quodlibeta* 1, q. 3, 13: 'Ita quod dum una eius pars fit, altera transit. Et ita quod nulla eius pars sit tota simul, quia nulla pars eius fit in instanti.'
[95] Jeck, *Aristoteles contra Augustinum*, 418.
[96] Jeck, *Aristoteles contra Augustinum*, 418.
[97] See Flasch's discussion of Vital in *Was ist Zeit?*
[98] Vital du Four, *Vitalis de Furno, Quodlibeta Tria*, ed. Ferdinand M. Delorme O.F.M. (Rome: Antonianum, 1947), 221.

through an instant. Since past and future do not exist in any way, he reasons, they cannot be continuous with any instant. Rather, 'time is composed and made continuous by instants, not as discrete existing entities, but through the continuous transition of these instants from potentiality to actuality.'[99] These instants succeed one another in complete continuity without any discrete separation.

In Vital's opinion, this nullifies Aristotle's view that the parts of time are joined together by a common boundary, namely, the instant. As Vital notes, the boundary must exist either in potency or in act. But if it is actual, then it would not be continuous in the way that time clearly is. Rather, time would be broken into two by the boundary itself. If the boundary is potential, however, then time is not really divided by it except in the imagination. Although the instant may be something discrete in our minds, consequently, Vital concludes that its continuous transition from potentiality to actuality ultimately creates continuity in time, which is subject to a constant flow.

Richard of Middleton

Richard of Middleton (1249–1302) was a particularly creative Franciscan author who studied in Paris and was part of the committee that evaluated Olivi's works in 1283. Like many others in his era, he discusses what time is and the nature of the instant in the context of inquiring whether angels are in time.[100] On his account, 'time is the continuation of motion by either duration or delay. [This continuation] is measured by the soul. By means of motion, which is its [the soul's] passion, the soul measures the continuation or duration of other motions.'[101] As Richard notes, Aristotle explicitly denies that time is identical with motion, since motion can be fast or slow, but time is only short or long. According to Richard, however, Aristotle also holds that it must be possible for time to be num-

---

99 Vital du Four, *Vitalis de Furno, Quodlibeta Tria*, 221: 'Sed componitur et continuatur ex instantibus non quidem existentibus discretis, quia hoc improbat Aristoteles, nec existentibus maioribus, sed per continuum exitum de potentia ad actum ipsorum instantium; succedunt enim alteri per continuationem talem sine aliqua discretione; est enim vera definitio continuorum sive continui, quod continuum est indiscretio quaedam cum potentia terminandi.'
100 Richardus de Mediavilla, *Super Quatuor Libros Sententiarum, Tomus Secundus* (Brixiae, 1591), d. 2, a. 1, q. 1, 31.
101 Richardus de Mediavilla, *Super Quatuor Libros Sententiarum*, d. 2, a. 1, q. 1, resp., 31: 'Dico ergo primo quod tempus est continuatio seu duratione seu mora motus ab anima numerata, qua mediante motu, cuius est passio mensurat anima continuationes vel durationes motuum aliorum.'

bered by the soul, which reduces time to discrete moments that make up the continuum of motion which we call time. As Richard elaborates:

> An instant is something indivisible, having a connection to time not as a part of time, but as the beginning or end of time, from which, without real discontinuation of time, the parts of time are measured by the soul. And all this can be derived from the words of the philosopher. But the instant, which is the end of the past and the beginning of the future, is not actually in time, because then time would really be discontinuous; rather, it is only in time potentially, or as it is signified actually by some apprehensive power, imaginably or intelligibly.[102]

On the grounds that the soul makes this signification by looking at the mobile, Richard acknowledges that some scholars argue that the instant follows the mobile object by which it is carried and thus remains the same in essence for all time, just as the moving object remains the same. Others however affirm that the instant remains the same in essence for all time while varying in its mode of existence as it moves through time. For his part, however, Richard reiterates that the instant is the measure of the motion of the mobile, and in virtue of this constant motion, it is disposed to progress in or fall out of being.[103] Thus, it is neither one and the same 'now' that flows through time, nor one 'now' that simply varies in its mode of existence. For Richard, in summary, the now is not a real entity but only a product the imagination which measures the flow of time.[104]

---

[102] Richardus de Mediavilla, *Super Quatuor Libros Sententiarum*, d. 2, a. 1, q. 1, resp., 31: 'Instans est aliquid indivisibile, habens connexionem ad tempus, non pars temporis, sed initium temporis, vel terminus, a quo sine reali discontinuatione temporis, partes temporis ab anima numerantur. Et hec omnia trahi possunt ex dictis Philosophum. Instans autem quod est terminus praeteriti et initium futuri non est in tempore actualiter et realiter discontinuaretur; sed est tantum in tempore potentialiter, vel aliqua vi apprehensiva actualiter signatum imaginabiliter vel intelligibiliter.'

[103] Richardus de Mediavilla, *Super Quatuor Libros Sententiarum*, d. 2, a. 1, q. 1, resp., 31: 'Ex praedictis patet quod instans est mensura mobilis sub ratione, qua mobile: et si est mobile, tali motu quo disponatur ad proficiendum inesse vel ad defectum essendi, sicut mensuratur ab instanti quod realiter differret ab instanti aevi.'

[104] As Richard reiterates in the next question, q. 2, resp., 32: 'Tempus est continuatio motus ab anima numerata.' 'Time is defined as the continuation of motion, measured by the soul.' In this connection, Richard – who is often more open than other Franciscans about his debt to Avicenna – cites the Islamic philosopher's *Metaphysics* 9.1 where he says 'this is what we call time, namely, the priority or measurement which lacks a location or stability but exists according to the way of succession. Therefore, wherever there is succession, there is time.', contra, 38: 'Hoc est quod nos vocamus tempus, scilicet, prioritatem vel mensurationem non habentem situm, nec stabilitatem, sed esse secundum viam successionis. Ergo ubicunque est successio ibi est tempus.'

William of Ockham

Like Scotus, William of Ockham (1287–1347) became the founder of his own 'school' of Franciscan thought which won advocates in the medieval universities for many generations. In his own lifetime, however, he was a controversial figure who conflicted with the Pope about the nature of Franciscan poverty. As a result, he never received the title of 'master of theology' for his studies in this area at Oxford. A prolific philosopher as well as theologian, Ockham discusses time in a number of places, including his *Sentences* commentary;[105] his commentary on Aristotle's *Physics*;[106] his *Summula Philosophiae Naturalis*;[107] and his *Quaestiones in libros Physicorum Aristotelis*.[108]

The accounts he offers in these different contexts in most respects overlap. Following Shapiro, I will take the Summula as the basis for my discussion in what follows but will cross-reference to the other texts by Ockham on time as relevant. In this Summula, Ockham begins his discussion of time with an explanation of what time is not.[109] In this regard, he writes:

> Concerning the instant, many hold the opinion that the instant is a certain flowing thing that immediately perishes or ceases, so that it does not endure. Hence, some posit that one instant after another continually comes to be, and that the instant is a certain entity for which it is impossible for to endure through time, and moreover, that it is distinguished from any permanent thing.[110]

---

[105] William of Ockham, *Quaestiones in Librum secundum Sententiarum (Reportatio)*, in *Guillelmi de Ockham, Opera Theologica*, vol. 5, ed. Gédeon Gal, Rega Wood (St Bonaventure, NY: Franciscan Institute Press, 1981), q. 10, 183–231.

[106] William of Ockham, *Expositio in Libros Physicorum Aristoteles, Libri IV-VIII*, ed. Vladimir Richter, Gerhard Leibold, Rega Wood (St Bonaventure, NY: Franciscan Institute Press, 1985), ch. 18–27, 194–316.

[107] William of Ockham, *Brevis Summa Libri Physicorum, Summula Philosophiae Naturalis et Quaestiones in Libros Physicorum Aristoteles*, in *Opera Philosophica*, vol. 6, ed. Stephen Brown (St Bonaventure, NY: Franciscan Institute Press, 1984): *Summula*, lib. 4, ch. 1–16, 344–390.

[108] William of Ockham, *Quaestiones in Libros Physicorum Aristoteles*, ed. Brown, q. 37, 493; cf. q. 57, 549.

[109] Herman Shapiro, *Motion, Time and Space According to William Ockham* (St Bonaventure, NY: The Franciscan Institute, 1957), 91–111. William of Ockham, *Summula*, lib. 4, ch. 1, 345: 'Sed quod instans non sit talis res ostendo primo, quia si instans sit talis res, sequeretur quod in quolibet tempore essent res infinitae, secundum se totas distinctae non facientes unum, productae et corruptae, quia in quolibet tempore quodlibet instans esset secundum se totum distinctum a quolibet alio et non faciunt unum, et infinita instantia sunt in quolibet tempore, igitur etc.'

[110] William of Ockham, *Summula*, lib. 4, ch. 1, 344–5: 'Circa instans autem est multorum opinio quod instans est quaedam res fluens quae statim corrumpitur vel desinit, ita quod non manet.

This view is objectionable in Ockham's opinion because it entails that any period of time would have to be comprised of infinite distinct entities, that is, discrete instants, which would disrupt the unity of time.[111] Another problem with this view is that it fails to explain how one moment ceases to be so that another can arise. This cessation would require that the instant either ends due to the introduction of its contrary, or the removal of its cause, or the corruption of the subject, none of which is the case for time. After rejecting the view of time as a kind of 'flowing now' which entails a constantly changing instant, Ockham moves on to develop his own account of time, which he defines in terms of the motion of permanent objects.[112] Thus, Ockham writes in his *Sentences* commentary that 'time is not something absolute, distinct in reality from permanent things and from motion.'[113]

In elaborating his account, Ockham specifies that time is the measure of the duration of the motions and rests of temporal things.[114] This measure can be taken on account of the constant and uniform movement of the first motion, namely, of the sun, by which we know that one thing moves or rests for longer or shorter periods than another.[115] According to Ockham, this understanding of time is consistent with Aristotle's view that 'time is the number of motion according to before and after,'[116] because if we were not able to see that a uniformly moving object (i.e. the sun) was first in one place and then in another, we would never be able to judge how long anything else rests, moves, or endures.[117]

Unde ponunt nonulli quod continue fit aliud et aliud instans et quod est res quaedam quam impossibile est permanere per tempus, immo quod distinguimur ab omni re permanente.'
111 Shapiro, *Motion, Time and Space*, 92.
112 William of Ockham, *Summula*, lib. 4, ch. 2, 349: 'Item, ostensum est quod motus non est res secundum se totam distincta a rebus permanentibus, igitur eadem ratione nec tempus.'
113 William of Ockham, *Sent.* II., q. 10, ar. 1, 185: 'Ad quaestionem igitur primo probo quod tempus non est aliquid absolutum distinctum realiter a rebus permanentibus et a motu.'
114 William of Ockham, *Summula*, lib. 4, ch. 2, 352: 'Cum igitur tempus secundum omnes sit mensura rerum temporalium et motuum et quietum, illa res erit tempus per quam de duratione rerum temporalium et duratione motuum et quietum certificamur.' See also William of Ockham, *Quaestiones in Libros Physicorum Aristoteles*, ed. Brown, q. 40, 502–4.
115 William of Ockham, *Summula*, lib. 4, ch. 2, 353: 'Ad hoc enim sufficit motus: si enim consideremus motum de quo scimus quod uniformis est, hoc est scimus quod tale motum semper movetur uniformiter, id est semper acque velociter, per hoc poterimus scire quod una res diutius alia vel minus diu movetur vel quiescit.' See also William of Ockham, *Quaestiones in Libros Physicorum Aristoteles*, ed. Brown, q. 42, 507–10.
116 William of Ockham, *Quaestiones in Libros Physicorum Aristoteles*, ed. Brown, q. 47, 524–6.
117 William of Ockham, *Summula*, lib. 4, ch. 2, 4, 354: 'Unde nisi cognosceremus quod mobile uniformiter prius esset in tali loco et posterius in alio, numquam possemus cognoscere nec per ipsum iudicare quamdiu aliud movetur vel quiescit vel durat.'

In explaining how 'number' factors into the definition of time, Ockham observes that Aristotle posited two possible understandings of number, namely, as that which is numbered and that by which we number.[118] For Ockham, time is that which is numbered (a 'numbered number') not that by which we number, because it consists of the numbered parts of the motion of an actual object. Here Ockham infers that time is comprised of discrete moments which are numbered by the soul that divides motion into prior and posterior parts.[119]

These parts do not disrupt the continuity of time, however, because time is essentially motion and inseparable from permanent objects in motion. Motion moreover is continuous, insofar as a movable object moves without rest between one place and another.[120] Thus, Ockham concludes that time must be continuous as well. Although Ockham thus identifies time with motion, he denies that every motion is time, because not every motion is that by which the motions can be measured. As Ockham thus concludes, time and motion have different definitions, even though they are closely intertwined.[121]

Ockham addresses numerous possible objections to his view that time is essentially motion. An obvious one is that motion can be fast or slow, but time cannot be fast or slow but rather long or short.[122] In his *Sentences* commentary, Ockham reckons with this problem by distinguishing between time taken according to the meaning of the term or according to the nature of what it is. In the first way, he reasons, time denotes a measure which is neither fast nor slow but regular and uniform.[123] In the second way, however, time is the same as motion and can therefore be perceived as fast or slow, because these qualities pertain to it insofar as it is subject to succession of moments that follow one another.[124]

Another important objection Ockham addresses concerns his claim that the instant is basically identical with the prime mobile. This would seem to conflict with the idea that instants succeed one another and are thus constantly generated and corrupted. Against this idea, Ockham argues that the instant tracks the changes in the location or position of the prime mobile.[125]

---

[118] William of Ockham, *Quaestiones in Libros Physicorum Aristoteles*, ed. Brown, q. 47, 524–6.
[119] William of Ockham, *Quaestiones in Libros Physicorum Aristoteles*, ed. Brown, q. 53, 538–40.
[120] William of Ockham, *Quaestiones in Libros Physicorum Aristoteles*, ed. Brown, q. 52, 537.
[121] William of Ockham, *Summula*, lib. 4, ch. 6, 357; cf. ch. 11, 372.
[122] William of Ockham, *Summula*, lib. 4, ch. 12, 373.
[123] William of Ockham, *Sent.* II., q. 10, ar. 2, 223; cf. William of Ockham, *Quaestiones in Libros Physicorum Aristoteles*, ed. Brown, q. 43, 512–14.
[124] William of Ockham, *Sent.* II., q. 10, ar. 2, 224.
[125] William of Ockham, *Summula*, lib. 4, ch. 12, 375–9.

The final question Ockham addresses concerns the relationship of time to the soul.[126] On the one hand, Ockham argues that time exists outside the soul because it principally involves the motion of the prime mobile, by which the inferior motions of temporal objects are measured. On the other hand, the actual measuring of those motions cannot take place without the soul knowing them, and thus the soul is important in Ockham's view for 'completing' the definition of time. As Ockham writes:

> The soul needs to be included in the definition of time, or rather, more properly speaking, the name of the soul, because measure is included in the definition of time. But measure in its definition includes the soul, because measure is that by which the soul must be made certain about an unknown quantity, as explained earlier. And so the soul must be included in the definition expressing what the name of time signifies, as it was in Aristotle's definition, which is: 'Time is the measure of motion according to the before and after.' This should be understood as: time is that by which the soul counts according to the before and after, through which it becomes certain about other things, how long they last, move, or rest.[127]

In light of this consideration, Ockham concludes that although 'time is truly outside the soul and does not really depend on the soul, time cannot be time unless it can be measured by the soul.'[128] This is a theme that Ockham further pursues at length in both his *Sentences* and physics commentaries. In the former, he argues that the principal meaning of time entails that it exists outside the soul and would exist even if there were no soul, because it signifies real motions which occur in things, and above all, the motion of the prime mobile. However, the complete meaning of time does involve the soul because it connotes the act of the soul enumerating time. As Ockham elaborates in his physics commentary, time exists in potency without the soul when it is considered as the motion of the heavens, which takes place regardless of whether the soul is aware of it. However, time can-

---

126 William of Ockham, *Summula*, lib. 4, ch. 15, 387–8.
127 William of Ockham, *Summula*, lib. 4, ch. 15, 387: 'Patet autem ex praedictis quod in definitione temporis debet anima poni, vel magis proprie loquendo nomen animae, quia in definitione temporis ponitur mensura. Sed mensura in definitione sua recipit animam, quia mensura est illud per quod anima debet certificari de quantitate ignota, modo praeexposito. Et ita anima debet poni in definitione exprimente quid nominis temporis, et ita fuit in definitione Aristotelis, quae est quod "tempus est numerus motus secundum prius et posterius." Quae debet sic intelligi: tempus est illud quo anima numerat secundum prius et posterius, per quod nata est certificari de aliis quantum durant, moventur vel quiescunt.'
128 William of Ockham, *Summula*, lib. 4, ch. 15, 389: 'Patet igitur quod tempus est realiter extra animam, nec dependet realiter ab anima; tamen tempus non posset esse tempus sive illud quod est tempus non posset esse tempus sine anima;' cf. *Sent.* II, q. 10, ar. 2, 194.

not exist in actuality *as time*, that is, as the numbering of motion, without the soul which performs the act of measuring time.[129]

Conclusion

In light of the foregoing, we can draw some conclusions about the Franciscans' understanding of time and the relationship between time and eternity. The first issue is best addressed by initially reviewing briefly the accounts of time considered so far. Aristotle's views on time were foundational for further thinkers like Avicenna and the Franciscans, who were constrained to reconcile their views at least with his language, even though their accounts of time ultimately differed from his considerably. According to Aristotle, time is what subsists between two points, one of which comes 'before' and the other, 'after'.

This 'middle' is the 'now' of the present moment. The passage of time involves the progression and indeed counting of these 'nows' or discrete moments that come one after another. Aristotle acknowledges that the now 'flows' in the sense that every moment in time is characterized by a 'now' which nonetheless differs at different points in time. For him, therefore, the 'flow' is essentially a series of discrete entities or instants. In that sense, Aristotle offers what we have described as a 'static' account of time, in which time is represented by the instant or that space between the before and after.

By contrast, Avicenna offers a dynamic account of time as a continuous or 'flowing' now. To do this, he takes as his point of departure Aristotle's insight that 'time is the number of motion when differentiated into earlier and later parts.' However, he draws from this claim the conclusion that Aristotle had rejected, namely, that time is essentially a kind of motion, given that 'before' and 'after' are necessary concomitants of motion. The motion in question, Avicenna elaborates, is that of the 'now', which can be considered in two ways: either as the boundary between the future and the past, that is, as a kind of discrete instant; or, in relation to its natural state of motion, where it is always flowing and thus producing the continuum of time. This is the proper way of considering the now, namely, as a single entity moving through time which nonetheless varies in its mode of being.

The *Summa Halensis* follows Avicenna in distinguishing between two ways of understanding the 'now' of time, one improper, and one proper. The improper way of conceiving time concerns the 'now' insofar as it is the boundary between the

---

[129] William of Ockham, *Quaestiones in Libros Physicorum Aristoteles*, ed. Brown, q. 49, 428–32.

past and future, that is, the beginning of the future and the end of the past. So construed, the 'now' represents a discrete moment. While some medieval scholars followed Aristotle in arguing that time is a succession of such discretions, the Summa insists that time is properly described as a continuous flow or motion of the 'now'.

As Avicenna had argued, so the Summa affirms that the 'now' is one and the same at every moment in time, since it basically moves continuously through time. Nevertheless, it differs according to the flow of time itself. In the same way that a mobile object remains one and the same throughout its motion, the Summa concludes that the 'now' is a singular entity that flows from one point in time to another and so creates time's continuity. Thus, the Summa adheres to Avicenna's idea of a dynamic or 'flowing' now, whose motion is the basis of time, which in turn tracks the duration of motion.

In his commentary on Aristotle's metaphysics, Scotus also advocated this idea of the 'flowing now' which remains the same in essence but differs according to its mode of existence as it moves through time. The analogy Scotus uses to explain this view is that of a point which is immutable or the same according to essence when it is at rest, but mutable insofar as it moves and creates a line through its flow. In his *Ordinatio*, by contrast, Scotus moves away from this idea of a 'flowing now'. He argues that the 'now' considered according to substance would be a sort of indivisible entity which cannot change or move, since it always remains exactly what it is. On this basis, Scotus concludes that the now is different in essence at every point in time, which in his view is a kind of motion, even though not every motion is time.

Olivi picks up where Scotus left off, inquiring whether time is the same as the 'flowing now' advocated by the *Summa Halensis*. Olivi rejects the idea that time consists of a single 'now' that flows, however, arguing that the 'now' does not actually exist except at the beginning and end of time, just as no point exists in a line except at its two termini. To support this claim, Olivi elaborates that time is essentially motion, or the measure of its duration, and no 'end' of motion like the 'now' can exist simultaneously with the motion itself. The idea that time is motion also serves as the basis for Olivi's claim that time exists outside the soul, since motion is something external to the mind. Ultimately, Olivi echoes Scotus in affirming that the 'now' cannot move because it always remains the same thing and is therefore incompatible with the constant flow of time.

Vital du Four mainly reiterates the views of his predecessors, indicating that time is co-extensive with motion, and in particular, the actualization of one moment after another. He contests the idea that time is merely an instant which is the boundary between the future and the past on the grounds that locating such a discrete moment in time would break the continuum of time into two. Richard of Middleton invokes this same argument, following his forebears in claiming that the instant is in constant motion and thus is always in a state of falling out of being. On this basis, he concludes that neither one and the same 'now' flows through time nor does it vary simply in its mode of existence.

The 'now' for Richard is not a real entity but only a product of the mind that measures the flow of time. Like his forebears, consequently, Richard denies that the 'now' represents the boundary between the past and future, because specifying such a boundary, to wit, the 'now', would render time discontinuous. Ockham also objects to the notion of a 'flowing now' on the grounds that time so construed would be comprised of infinite discrete entities, which would disrupt the unity and flow of time.

The concept of a 'flowing now' is also problematic in his view because it cannot explain how one moment ceases to be so that another can arise. On this basis, Ockham boldly asserts that time is inseparable from permanent objects which are in motion and thus from motion itself. Indeed, time for him simply measures the duration of the motion of objects. According to Ockham, this view is consistent with the Aristotelian notion elucidated by Avicenna that time numbers what comes before and what comes after.

As the foregoing summary confirms, consequently, Franciscans adhered to the fundamentally Avicennian insight that time is a kind of motion, even though they differed in how they did so. For the later Franciscan thinkers particularly, it is inconsistent with the very idea of what time is to locate discrete moments in time, let alone to count them as Aristotle did, because this would disrupt the constant flow which is essential to what time is, namely, the flow of the present from the future into the past.

The question that remains to address in light of this is whether the Franciscan account of time was deliberately paired with, or even followed from, the moderate understanding of God as 'everlasting' which they also advocated. The hypothesis of this study is that there is indeed a relationship between Franciscan accounts of time and God's relationship to time, just as there seems to be a connection between more 'static' accounts of time which number a series of 'present moments' and the notion of God as an eternal being who sees all things in his 'eternal now'.

The focus in the latter context is on the 'now' of the present moment, both in God's eternal knowledge and for humans who are subject to the constraints of time. The difference is that God's 'now' contains the past and the future as if in the present, whereas for us those temporal categories remain. We must therefore move from present moment to present moment in succession in order to know what is eternally present to God.

In the Franciscan account of time, by contrast, the focus is not on the 'now' or on counting 'nows' but on the continuum of time as a whole and its fundamental

Conclusion

state of motion. This more dynamic way of construing time relates more naturally to a view of God who is somehow able to track with the motion of time, even though he himself is outside of time and thus does not move. In that sense, we can see why the early Franciscans preferred to describe God as a being of 'infinite duration', namely, because he is the ultimate arbiter of the duration of motion which it is the purpose of time to measure.

In what follows, we will discover the impact this way of thinking about God and his relationship to time had in the Franciscan way of conceiving of God's knowledge of temporal categories and especially the future, which is not accessible to our knowledge but presumably is to his. Here I will focus a bit more narrowly on the theories of the *Summa Halensis*, Scotus, and Ockham, which represents key moments in the development of the Franciscan tradition of thinking on this matter.

God's Knowledge of Future Contingents

The *Summa Halensis* on Future Contingents

The problem of explaining how God can foreknow the future without determining it was a longstanding question in the history of ideas, which in the Western tradition has its roots principally in Aristotle, Augustine, and Boethius, among others. As we have seen already, proponents of divine eternity tended to resolve the question by affirming that God knows future contingents as if they were eternally present to him. As Gloria Frost helpfully indicates, however, Franciscan thinkers tended to favour a different approach to conceiving God's knowledge of the future, which 'bases God's knowledge of contingents on his knowledge of his own causation of them.'[1]

This approach arguably draws inspiration from Avicenna, who also claimed that God knows all things including future contingents through himself as the cause of everything. On the basis of this understanding, early Franciscans similarly argued that God knows from eternity all that he will bring about or permit to occur at any point in time, including in the future. Thus, his knowledge makes reference to the temporal moment when from our point of view his causality takes effect, even though it is eternal in its own right. This view emerges clearly in the question the Summa addresses whether God's foreknowledge is temporal or eternal.[2] In answering this question, the Summa states that:

> Foreknowledge implies [something] eternal, nevertheless with respect to the temporal. For eternity can be described as either absolute or relative. Absolutely, [God's] knowledge implies [something] eternal; but foreknowledge implies [something] eternal in a qualified or relative sense. Thus, it must be said that foreknowledge posits a thing in its cause, nevertheless, in respect to the temporal. For it posits things which will be in the knowledge of God. Thus, it must be said that antecedence implies [something] eternal, but in respect to the temporal, while knowledge implies [something] eternal absolutely.[3]

---

[1] Gloria Frost, 'Divine Power, Knowledge and Will,' in *The Oxford Handbook of Medieval Franciscan Thought*, ed. Drew Rosato, Lydia Schumacher (Oxford: Oxford University Press, forthcoming). Frost also points to an important passage which makes the point that God knows contingents in terms of himself as cause: *SH* 1, P1, IN1, Tr5, S2, Q1, 248.

[2] *SH* 1, P1, IN1, Tr5, S2, Q1, C1, 266.

[3] *SH* 1, P1, IN1, Tr5, S2, Q1, C1, Respondeo, 267: 'Est loqui de re aeterna multipliciter. Quaedam enim dicuntur de re aeterna, quae Deus est, ut sine principio et sine fine: ut eum dicitur "Deus est iustus, bonus, sapiens", quia sine initio et sine fine bonus est. Quaedam dicuntur ut cum principio et cum fine, ut cum dicitur "Deus creat hanc animam"; Deus enim non ab aeterno creavit hanc animam nec semper creat eam. Quaedam vero dicuntur de eo ut cum principio, sed tamen sine

The key point the Summa makes here is that 'foreknowledge posits a thing in its cause, nevertheless, in respect to the temporal.' This means that, so far as it concerns the divine cause himself, God's knowledge is eternal, but with respect to the creature known, his knowledge pertains to a temporal matter, namely, something which will occur in the future. In replying to the objections raised against this viewpoint, the Summa makes a number of additional key observations about divine foreknowledge. First of all, in response to the claim that God's foreknowledge ceases when a future contingent comes to pass, the Summa holds that this does not imply any change in God, because what changes is only the relation of a creature to God. To illustrate this point, the Summa cites the example of a person who moves from my right side to my left side. While this move alters their relation to me, it does not cause a change in me personally.[4]

According to the Summa, this is how it is with God's foreknowledge, which principally concerns the idea of a future thing in God. Although the idea ceases to be an idea of the future when the event it prefigures comes to pass, it does not cease to be the idea of the event in God. Thus, the Summa confirms that the occurrence of an event God foreknew does not bring about change in God but only in the temporal status of the object, which was once future and is then present and then past.[5] This changing status is something that God's knowl-

---

fine, ut cum dicitur "Deus est dominator"; hoc enim non dicitur de Deo ab aeterno, quia antequam esset creatura, non potuit hoc dici: "dominator" enim dicit illum cui subiectus est aliquis; dicitur ergo "dominator" ex tempore, tamen sine fine, quia creatura, cui dominatur, est sine fine. Sicut ergo non est inconveniens aliqua dici de Deo cum principio et cum fine, et quaedam ut cum principio, tamen sine fine, sic non est inconveniens ponere alterum, scilicet quod quaedam dicuntur de Deo ut sine principio, tamen cum fine, ut praescientia. Ad illud ergo quod quaeritur utrum praescientia sit aeterna vel temporalis: dicendum quod praescientia dicit aeternum, tamen in respectu ad temporale. Est ergo loqui de aeterno absolute vel in comparatione. Absolute, scientia dicit aeternum; praescientia vero dicit aeternum in respectu vel in comparatione. Dicendum ergo quod praescientia ponit res in causa, tamen in respectu ad temporale: unde ponit res quae erunt in scientia Dei. Dicendum ergo quod antecessio dicit aeternum, sed in in respectu ad temporale, sed scientia dicit aeternum absolute.'
4 *SH* 1, P1, IN1, Tr5, S2, Q1, C1, Ad objecta 1, 267: 'Ad illud quod obicitur "nihil quod desinit est aeternum" etc.: dicendum quod non valet. Aliquid enim dicitur desinere, non propter mutationem quae fit in ipso, sed propter mutationem quae est in alio: sicut possum esse dexter et sinister sive desinere esse dexter et incipere esse sinister, me non mutato; ut posito quod unus modo sit a parte una mei, modo ab alia; dicitur ergo desitio tantum propter respectum qui est ad alterum, non propter mutationem quae sit facta in me. Similiter dicendum de praescientia, quod dicitur desinere non propter ipsam scientiam; sed propter ipsum respectum, quia ipsa res, ad quam est respectus, mutatur vel desinit.'
5 *SH* 1, P1, IN1, Tr5, S2, Q1, C1, Ad objecta 3, 267: 'Item, ad illud quod obicitur quod "nihil est Deo futurum, et praescientia dicitur respect futuri" etc.: dicendum quod futurum in praescientia Dei

edge is able to 'track', precisely because the changes in question do not occur in him but in the object of his knowledge, of which he is the cause.

After thus establishing that God foreknows temporal things in virtue of himself as their cause, the Summa proceeds to pose the traditional Lombardian questions whether God's knowledge is the cause of or is caused by temporal things, including our free choices. The author gives a somewhat standard answer to the first question, namely, that God's foreknowledge signifies only antecedence but not causality.[6] In other words, the necessity of God's knowledge of the future only entails that he necessarily knows in advance what will happen, not that he imposes necessity on contingent things, as if compelling them to happen.[7]

To reinforce this point, the Summa invokes Boethius' distinction between the absolute necessity of things that have an inevitable or determined cause, like the sun rising tomorrow, or a conditional necessity, where the necessity follows what occurs. For example, if I sit down, it is necessary that I sit down.[8] While the first kind of necessity is indeed incompatible with contingencies and thus with human free will, the latter type is not.

Likewise, the Summa denies that foreknown objects can be the cause of God's knowledge, insofar as the *fore* in foreknowledge refers to the status of the knowable thing from our temporal point of view, not to God's knowledge as such, which is not subject to temporal categories.[9] On these grounds, the Summa claims that the temporal is not the cause of the eternal but only the reason why it is called 'future' by us. As the Summa elaborates in a discussion of the infallibility of God's foreknowledge:

---

nihil aliud est quam idea rei futurae in Deo; idea autem desinit esse idea, prout dicitur rei futurae, ex quo ideatum est, nec tamen desinit id quod est idea, tamen desinit esse idea huius, id est futuri. Similiter id quod est praescientia non desinit, tamen esse in ratione praescientiae desinit: et hoc est in ratione respectus connotati. Similiter dicendum quod veritas mundi futuri nihil aliud est quam ratio mundi future quae ratio non desinit esse simpliciter, sed desini esse futuri: unde sicut nummus incipit et desinit esse pretium sine sui mutatione, ita praescientia desinit esse praescientia sui mutatione.'

6 *SH* 1, P1, IN1, Tr5, S2, Q1, C2, 268–9. Interestingly, these are the only three questions about foreknowledge that Bonaventure poses in his major *Sentences* commentary, which briefly repeats the solutions to these questions offered by the *Summa Halensis*. Bonaventure, *In librum primum Sententiarum*, in *Opera omnia*, Tome 2 (Paris: Vivès 1864), d. 38, 62–75. Bonaventure, *Sententiae* I, d. 38, trans. Richard E. Houser, Timothy B. Noone, *Commentary on the Sentences: Philosophy of God* (St Bonaventure, NY: The Franciscan Institute, 2014), 223–47.

7 *SH* 1, P1, IN1, Tr5, S2, Q1, C4, Respondeo, 270.

8 *SH* 1, P1, IN1, Tr5, S2, Q1, C4, Ad objecta 1, 270. Boethius, *Consolation of Philosophy*, 5.6.

9 *SH* 1, P1, IN1, Tr5, S2, Q1, C3, Ad objecta 3, 269.

This phrase 'God does not know the past as past' has a dual meaning: this determination 'as past' can specify the verb in comparison to the knower, and in this sense, it is true, because the past does not exist in God in the mode of the past, but in his own mode; or it can specify the verb in comparison to the known, and in this sense, it is false: God indeed knows past things and things that are under the condition of pastness and futureness, but he does not know them under these conditions, but eternally and presently. Similarly, in response to that phrase 'God knows things differently than they are': this has a dual meaning, because this determination 'differently' can specify the verb in relation to two things. If in relation to the known, it is false; if in relation to the knower, it is true. Indeed, what is comprehended exists in the comprehender according to the mode of the comprehender, not according to the mode of the thing comprehended.[10]

In this context, the Summa follows Alexander of Hales in distinguishing the term 'foresee' from the term 'create', noting that the latter implies an actual effect or relation to a creature in time.[11] By contrast, God's foreknowledge only refers to the potential latent in God's eternal knowledge for a being to exist in the future from our point of view. Although the Summa thus continues to affirm that God knows what he knows in a way that befits his eternity, its tendency to reconstrue eternity in terms of everlastingness, that is, God's presence to all times or all times as present to him, nevertheless leads to a greater stress on the sense in which God is able to know past and future things by virtue of himself as their cause. Precisely what it means that he knows temporal things in an eternal way is not really a matter the Summa fully clarifies, however. Thus, it remained for later Franciscans like Scotus and Ockham to try to develop the teaching on future contingents further.

---

10 *SH* 1, P1, IN1, Tr5, S2, Q1, C6, Ad objecta 3, 272: 'Ad aliud dicendum quod haec "Deus non scit praeterita ut praeterita": duplex est: quia haec determinatio "ut praeterita" potest determinare verbum in comparatione ad scientem, et sic vera, quia praeterita non sunt in Deo per modum praeteriti, sed per modum suum; vel potest determinare verbum in comparatione ad scitum, et sic falsa est: scit enim Deus res praeteritas et quae sunt sub conditione praeteritionis et futuritionis, sed non scit sub iis conditionibus, sed aeternaliter et praesentialiter. Similiter ad illud: Deus scit res aliter quam sunt: haec est duplex, quia haec determinatio "aliter" in duplici comparatione potest determinare verbum. Si in comparatione ad scitum, falsa est; si in comparatione ad scientem, vera. Quod enim comprehenditur est in comprehendente secundum modum ipsius, non secundum modum rei comprehensae.'
11 *SH* 1, P1, IN1, Tr5, S2, Q1, C7, Ad objecta 1, 274.

John Duns Scotus on Future Contingents

The *Ordinatio*

Over the course of his career, Duns Scotus offered several accounts of future contingents which are more or less consistent with one another.[12] The earliest can be found in his *Lectura*, but perhaps the most well-known appears in the second part of distinction 38 of his *Ordinatio*, which discusses the infallibility of divine knowledge.[13] This discussion continues into distinction 39, which treats the immutability of God's knowledge.[14] These sections are printed in an appendix to the Vatican edition because of questions about their authenticity.

As the Vatican editors observe, the *Ordinatio* material on future contingents was probably added by a scribe or follower of Scotus, who left blank pages in his own personal copy of the *Ordinatio* where these sections were meant to appear.[15] A number of scholars have taken this to mean that Scotus was not satisfied with some aspects of his earlier account in the *Lectura* and wanted to develop it further. In particular, Scotus apparently recognized that his theory could not explain how God knows future human free choices, since these are not subject to the determination of his will, which we will see below is decisive for his understanding of future contingents. As Gloria Frost demonstrates, this problem was particularly acute when it came to explaining how God knows human sins, since these are not willed but only permitted by God.[16]

Whereas the *Ordinatio* material was not revised by Scotus himself but is based on a student transcript of his lectures, the later account Scotus offered in his *Reportatio* on the Paris Lectures was revised by Scotus personally. Thus, it serves as an important source for his thinking on future contingents and will

---

[12] I am grateful to Gloria Frost for advice on formulating this passage.
[13] John Duns Scotus, *Contingency and Freedom, Lectura I 39*, ed. and trans. Antoine Vos, Henri Veldhuis, Aline H. Looman-Graanskamp, Eef Dekker, Nico W. den Bok (Dordrecht: Kluwer Academic Publishers, 1994).
[14] John Duns Scotus, *Opus Oxoniense* (*Ordinatio*) I, d. 38–39 in *Opera omnia*, vol. 6, ed. Karl Balić (Civitas Vaticana: Typis Polyglottia Vaticanis, 1963), Appendix A, 401
[15] John Duns Scotus, *Ordinatio* 1, ed. Balić, 26*–30*.
[16] Gloria Frost, 'John Duns Scotus on God's Knowledge of Sins: A Test-Case for God's Knowledge of Contingents,' *Journal of the History of Philosophy* 48:1 (2010), 25. Although Scotus later acknowledged that God knows future contingents such as sins, even when he has not willed them, Frost shows that he never explains precisely how God knows them.

be considered following the discussion of the *Ordinatio* below, although the two accounts are very similar.[17]

In question 38 of this text, Scotus starts by considering two main views of how God knows future contingents which he opposes. The first is the view that God knows future contingents in virtue of his divine ideas, which allow God to know all things that are or could be patterned after those ideas. In evaluating this position, Scotus stresses that all the knowledge God possesses by way of the divine ideas is natural, or prior to any act of his will, which means that it is necessary and cannot be otherwise.[18] On this basis, he argues that if God knew future contingents through his divine ideas, this would pre-determine future events and undermine their contingency, and along with it, the freedom of the will.[19]

Another view Scotus considers, clearly that of Aquinas, is that God knows future contingents by virtue of the fact that all times are present to him in eternity.[20] In response to this perspective, Scotus argues that God's immensity in relation to time – that is, his eternity – much like his relation to place – does not entail that he exists at any time – or place – except those that actually exist or are necessary.[21] As Scotus writes:

> The immensity of God would not be the reason for coexisting with any place (in some 'now') unless it is existing; for God does not coexist with any place by his immensity, except [with that] which exists in it [the universe], although he could cause a place outside the universe, and then by his immensity he would coexist with it. Therefore, if immensity is not the reason for coexisting with a place except if it is an actual one (and not a the potential one, because it

---

[17] William Craig, 'John Duns Scotus on God's Foreknowledge and Future Contingents,' *Franciscan Studies* 47 (1987), 98. Another detailed discussion of Scotus' writings on future contingents is provided by Allan B. Wolter, 'Scotus' Paris Lectures on God's Knowledge of Future Events,' in *The Philosophical Theology of John Duns Scotus*, ed. Marilyn McCord Adams, Allan B. Wolter (Ithaca: Cornell, 1990), 285–333.

[18] Duns Scotus, *Ordinatio* 1, ed. Balić, 38.1.6, 305: 'Si ante actum voluntatis divinae posset intellectus divinus aliquam talem cognitionem habere, habere team mere naturaliter et necessario, quia omnis cognitio praecedens ibi actum voluntatis est mere naturalis, et per essentiam ut est mere ratio naturalis intelligendi; de necessitate ergo cognosceret hoc esse faciendum, et tunc voluntas, cui hoc offeret, non posset non velle istud, quia tunc posset non essa recta potens discordare a ratione practica recta, et ita potest esse non recta.'

[19] Duns Scotus, *Ordinatio* 1, ed. Balić, 38.1.9, 306–7: 'Et ideo necesse est ponere primam determinationem in voluntate respect factibilium; non sic autem esset si intellectus practicus praedeterminaret, immo proprie libertas non posset salvari in voluntate respectu factibilium (sed nec contingentia aliqua), quia intellectus necessario praedeterminaret eam mera necessitate naturali et voluntas necessario conformaretur intellectui.'

[20] Duns Scotus, *Ordinatio* 1, ed. Balić, Appendix A, 38.2.B, 407.

[21] See Richard Cross, 'Duns Scotus on Eternity and Timelessness,' *Faith and Philosophy* 14:1 (1992), 3–25.

does not exist), by the same reasoning, eternity will not be the reason for coexisting with anything except if it exists; and this is what is argued, that 'that which does not exist, cannot coexist with anything', because 'coexisting' denotes a real relation, but a relation is not real unless its foundation is real.[22]

As Scotus concludes in this passage, God cannot co-exist with any times that do not exist, which is only the case for the present. This does not mean that there is no way in which Scotus thinks that God can know future contingents, however. To explain how this is possible, Scotus resorts to an explanation that invokes the divine will, which has access to certain *complexa* or subject-predicate statements such as 'I will sit tomorrow' or its opposite, 'I will not sit tomorrow'. While the intellect only knows these *complexa* in a neutral way, the divine will has the power to make one of the statements true and the other false.[23] Once it has done so, the divine intellect discovers what future events will transpire in virtue of its knowledge of the decisions of the divine will. As Scotus writes: 'the divine intellect, when seeing the determination of the divine will, sees that this thing will be at time A, because the will determines it will be at that time; for it knows the will is immutable and cannot be prevented.'[24] Since the divine will is contingent – it allows a proposition to remain either true or false up to the very moment of decision – it does not undermine the contingency of the future or determine the future course of events.

---

22 Duns Scotus, *Ordinatio* 1, ed. Balić, 38.2.B.9, 409: 'Immensitas tamen Dei non esset sibi ratio coexistendi alicui loco (in aliquo "nunc") nisi existenti; non enim Deus per immensitatem sui coexsistit alicui nisi quod est in illo, licet posset causare locum extra universum, et tunc per immensitatem suam illi coexisteret. Si ergo immensitas non est ratio coexistendi loco nisi actuali, et non potentiali (quia non est), pari ratione aeternitas non erit ratio coexistendi alicui nisi exsistenti; et hoc est quod arguitur quod "illud quod non est, nulli potest coexistere", quia "coexsistere" dicit relationem realem, sed relatio non est realis cuius fundamentum non est reale.'
23 Duns Scotus, *Ordinatio* 1, ed. Balić, 38.2.22, 428: 'Intellectus divinus aut offert simplicia quorum unio est contingens in re, aut, si complexionem, offert eam sicut sibi neutram; et voluntas eligens unam partem, scilicet coniunctionem istorum pro aliquo "nunc" in re, facit illud esse determinate verum: "hoc erit pro a". Hoc autem exsistente "determinate vero", essentia est ratio intellectui divino intelligendi istud verum, et hoc naturaliter (quantum est ex parte essentiae).'
24 Duns Scotus, *Ordinatio* 1, ed. Balić, 38.2.22, 428: 'Intellectus divinus, videndo determinationem voluntatis divinae, videt illud fore pro a, quia illa voluntas determinat fore pro eo; scit enim illam voluntatem esse immutabilem et non impedibilem.' See also Calvin Normore, 'Future Contingents,' in *The Cambridge History of Later Medieval Philosophy*, ed. Norman Kretzmann, Anthony Kenny, Jan Pinborg, Eleonore Stump (Cambridge: Cambridge University Press, 1982), 358–81.

The *Reportatio*

In his later *Reportatio*, Scotus re-iterates many aspects of the account that he had articulated earlier in his *Ordinatio*, elaborating some of them further.[25] As in that text, he initially considers the views of Aquinas and Henry of Ghent. The former argued that God knows future contingents in virtue of his 'eternal now', which 'embraces the whole of time and all of the temporal instances that characterize those things to which eternity is present.'[26] The latter claimed that God knows the future by way of his divine ideas, 'by means of which God sees all the conditions of things and all combinations between them.'[27] In describing Aquinas' view, Scotus distinguishes between two ways of understanding God's knowledge of future contingents, namely, God can know them either in themselves or in himself as cause.

The knowledge of a future contingent in itself does not entail knowledge of it as future or as contingent, in Scotus' view, because what is to be known is already determined. By contrast, the knowledge of a future contingent in its cause does entail knowing that it is future and contingent, because such knowledge does not presuppose that the outcome or effect has already been realized. According to Scotus, Aquinas holds that God knows future contingents not only in their cause but also in themselves, because the past, present, and future are all immediately present to him in his eternal act of understanding.

As we have seen in the *Ordinatio*, Scotus objects to this view on the grounds that 'God is not present through his immensity to any place unless that place actually exists.'[28] On this basis, Scotus concludes that 'God does not coexist through the eternal 'now' with any part of time except with this very now of the present.'[29] The reason Scotus gives here is that 'it is impossible for a real relation, namely, [a relation of] "being present" to be, or to be understood as, actual without the extremes [actually existing].'[30] As Scotus stresses, the real relation in question is not one of God to the creature but only of the creature to God.[31] Otherwise, the impli-

---

25 Joachim Roland Söder, *Kontingenz und Wissen. Die Lehre von den* futura contingentia *bei Johannes Duns Scotus* (Münster: Aschendorff Verlag, 1999) takes both texts into account and offers an edition of the *Reportatio* text as well.
26 John Duns Scotus, *The Examined Report of the Paris Lecture (Reportatio I-A)*, vol. 2, ed. and trans. Allan B. Wolter, Oleg V. Bychkov (St Bonaventure, NY: Franciscan Institute Publications, 2008), 450.
27 John Duns Scotus, *Reportatio I-A*, trans. Wolter/Bychkov, 455.
28 Duns Scotus, *Reportatio I-A*, trans. Wolter/Bychkov, 452.
29 Duns Scotus, *Reportatio I-A*, trans. Wolter/Bychkov, 452.
30 Duns Scotus, *Reportatio I-A*, trans. Wolter/Bychkov, 452.
31 Duns Scotus, *Reportatio I-A*, trans. Wolter/Bychkov, 245–49.

cation would be that God changes every time a creature comes into existence or that he depends upon creatures, which is impossible.³² Thus, Scotus writes:

> Every real relation has some real term as its object; however, in God [any] real relation must have existed from eternity, because no new realities occur in God in time: therefore, the creature acts as his real term from all eternity. Or, one can form an argument in the following way: that which is really related to something, depends on it for some [of its] real being; but God does not depend on the creature for any [of his] being; therefore, he is not really related to it.³³

Although Scotus thus rejects the real relation of God to his creatures, he allows that God is rationally related to creatures, both those that actually exist or those that could or will exist, by virtue of his eternal knowledge of himself as their cause.³⁴ According to Scotus, this knowledge entails that God is able to cognize how creatures were, are, or will be related to him, without himself being subject to temporal succession.³⁵ After all, Scotus understands God as a being of infinite duration who himself is not subject to change.³⁶

On this basis, Richard Cross affirms that Scotus upholds a B-series view, according to which there is no past, present, and future in God, contesting the claims of Craig who holds that Scotus' God is subject to the A-series.³⁷ At the same time, however, Cross acknowledges that Scotus' conception of eternity differs from that of Augustine and Aquinas who had effectively collapsed the past, present, and future into God's 'eternal now'. This is precisely because Scotus posits a rational relation to creatures, on account of which God co-exists with all times, which can in turn therefore be predicated of God. As Scotus writes:

> These terms [past, present, future] consignify the 'now' of eternity insofar as it coexists with the parts of time. For example, 'God begot [his Son]' con-signifies the 'now' of eternity, such

---

32 Duns Scotus, *Reportatio I-A*, trans. Wolter/Bychkov, 256–57: 'Every real relation has some real term as its object; however, in God [any] real relation must have existed from eternity, because no new realities occur in God in time: therefore, the creature acts as his real term from all eternity. Or, one can form an argument in the following way: that which is really related to something, depends on it for some [of its] real being; but God does not depend on the creature for any [of his] being; therefore, he is not really related to it.' On Scotus' understanding of relations, see Mark G. Henninger, *Relations: Medieval Theories 1250–1325* (Oxford: Clarendon Press, 1989), 68–97.
33 Duns Scotus, *Reportatio I-A*, trans. Wolter/Bychkov, 245–49.
34 Cross, 'Duns Scotus on Eternity,' 13–15.
35 See Marilyn McCord Adams, *William Ockham*, vol. 2 (Notre Dame: University of Notre Dame Press, 1989), 1123.
36 John Duns Scotus, *God and Creatures: The Quodlibetal Questions*, ed. Felix Alluntis, Allan B. Wolter (Princeton and London: Princeton University Press, 1975), 141–3.
37 Cross, 'Duns Scotus on Eternity,' 11.

that the sense is 'God has the act of generation in the 'now' of eternity in so far as that 'now' coexisted with the past'; and 'God begets' means the act of generation is in the 'now' of eternity in so far as it coexists with the present. Thus, since the now [of eternity] truly coexists with any difference of time, we can truly predicate of God the differences of all times.[38]

As Scotus stresses, God's co-existence with all times does not entail that he himself is subject to time but only confirms his awareness of how creatures are related to him in time. While Scotus and his Franciscan colleagues thus continue to affirm that God is timelessly eternal, consequently, the fact that God as a being of infinite or endless duration is able to know the temporal moments in which events occur already edges in the direction of a more moderate form of everlastingness which figures like Aquinas would roundly reject. After himself dismissing Aquinas' opinion, Scotus moves on to assess the view of Henry of Ghent, according to whom God knows future contingents 'because the ideas which God has of everything give him the exact picture of future things.'[39]

The problem with this view for Scotus is again that all knowledge is natural, that is, non-voluntary, and as a consequence, it is necessary. Thus, if God's knowledge of future contingents consisted in his ideas, 'he could not know the opposite of what he [already] knows, and as a consequence, the opposite could not occur. But this is false, because no future outcome is of itself necessary but only contingent.'[40] After thus assessing the views of Aquinas and Henry, Scotus proceeds to develop his own account of how God knows future contingents. This again turns heavily on his view of how God knows complexes, which are propositions composed of subject and predicate terms, such as 'Peter will be beatified' or 'Judas will be condemned'.[41]

---

[38] Cross, 'Duns Scotus on Eternity,' 15–16, quoting Duns Scotus, *Ordinatio* 1, in *Opera omnia*, vol. 4. (Civitas Vaticana: Typis Polyglottia Vaticanis, 1950), d. 1.9, n. 17, 336–37: 'Sed quid significant ista verba diversorum temporum, cum dicuntur de Deo? Respondeo. Magis proprie possunt dici consignificare "nunc" aeternitatis quam differentias temporis; nec tamen illud "nunc" absolute, quia non esset tunc variatio modorum diversorum temporis significandi sed in quantum coexsistit partibus temporis, ut cum dicitur: "Deus genuit", con-significatur "nunc" aeternitatis, ut sit sensus, Deus habet actum generationis in "nunc" aeternitatis in quantum illud "nunc" coexsistebat praeterito, "Deus generat", hoc est habet actum generationis in "nunc" aeternitatis in quantum coexsistit praesenti. Ex hoc patet quod cum illud "nunc" vere coexsistat cuilibet differentiae temporis, vere dicimus de Deo differentias omnium temporum.'
[39] Duns Scotus, *Reportatio I-A*, trans. Wolter/Bychkov, 450.
[40] Duns Scotus, *Reportatio I-A*, trans. Wolter/Bychkov, 456.
[41] Duns Scotus, *Reportatio I-A*, trans. Wolter/Bychkov, 457. Also see a very helpful discussion of Scotus' view of future contingents and complexa in Simo Knuuttila and Gloria Frost, 'Medieval Theories of Future Contingents,' *Stanford Encyclopedia of Philosophy*, https://plato.stanford.edu/archives/sum2025/entries/medieval-futcont, accessed 1 March 2025.

According to Scotus, God knows such complexes concerning possible future events in a way that is entirely neutral and does not entail their truth or falsity. Nevertheless, the divine intellect makes these propositions available to the divine will, which is able to choose whether to unite the terms or not to unite them.[42] In doing so, the will of God establishes the truth of one outcome and the falsity of its opposite, although the outcome itself remains contingent – like God's will itself – until it actually occurs. By virtue of knowing the contents of the divine will, consequently, the divine intellect comes to know what will happen in the future.[43] Here again, Scotus shows how God knows future contingents without rendering them necessary or inhibiting the human freedom of the will, which retains the power to choose between opposites at the very moment of willing.

Ockham on Future Contingents

As Normore observes, 'the position which rapidly became the *opinio communis* of the early fourteenth century was that worked out and defended by Ockham.'[44] The first question Ockham addresses on the topic of future contingents concerns the status of *complexa* like 'Peter is predestined' or 'Judas is reprobate.' Although such propositions concern the present, Ockham notes that they pertain to a future reward or punishment that God will give the individuals in question.[45] While statements about the present and past are always necessary, Ockham notes that statements about the future are contingent, because their truth value can change up until the moment the future becomes present.[46]

This raises the question for Ockham about the status of God's knowledge of future contingents. At face value, such knowledge, like divine knowledge in general, would seem to be true from eternity, in which case it is necessary and cannot be otherwise.[47] However, Ockham rejects this inference, reiterating that all future contingent propositions are by definition contingent and thus not true or false

---

42 Duns Scotus, *Reportatio I-A*, trans. Wolter/Bychkov, 458.
43 Duns Scotus, *Reportatio I-A*, trans. Wolter/Bychkov, 458.
44 Normore, 'Future Contingents,' 370.
45 William of Ockham, *Tractatus de praedestinatione et de praescientia Dei respectu futurorum contingentium*, ed. Philotheus Böhner, in *Opera Philosophica et Theologica*, vol. 1/2 (St Bonaventure, NY: The Franciscan Institute, 1978), q. 1, 508. Translated by Marilyn McCord Adams, Norman Kretzmann, *William Ockham: Predestination, God's Foreknowledge, and Future Contingents* (Indianapolis: Hackett, 1983), 37.
46 *William Ockham*, ed. Adams/Kretzmann, 38.
47 *William Ockham*, ed. Adams/Kretzmann, 40.

until the events to which they refer take place.[48] For this reason, Ockham concludes that statements like 'God predestined Peter from eternity' can turn out to be false even though they are true now.[49] In affirming this, Ockham argues against the position of Scotus, which he concisely summarizes as follows:

> The Subtle Doctor maintains that the divine intellect, insofar as it is in some respect prior to the determination of the divine will, apprehends those complexes as neutral [with respect to itself], and then the divine will determines that one part [of the contradiction] is true for some instant, willing that part is true for that same instant. After the determination of the divine will is effected, however, the divine intellect sees the determination of its own will, which is immutable. It sees clearly that one part is true with certainty – viz. that part which its own will wills to be true.[50]

According to Ockham, Scotus' position undermines the freedom of the human will, because this would be impeded by the prior act of the divine will, which could not help but pre-determine human choices in a necessary way. Furthermore, Ockham notes that locating God's foreknowledge in his will entails that God causes human beings to make their evil choices, which is not the case.[51] As Gloria Frost has shown, this is a problem Scotus himself recognized but was never able to resolve. With this issue in mind, Ockham reiterates that God cannot have certain or necessary knowledge of any future event that is still contingent, such as the exercise of the human will.

As Ockham writes: 'since the determination of the created will does not exist from eternity, God did not have certain cognition of the things that remained for a created will to determine.'[52] Despite affirming this, Ockham concedes that God must know the future, by virtue of his intuitive cognition, which makes all things

---

48 *William Ockham*, ed. Adams/Kretzmann, 43.
49 *William Ockham*, ed. Adams/Kretzmann, 43; ed. Böhner, 512–13: 'Unde quantumcumque istae modo sint verae ante beatitudinem datam Petro "Deus praedestinavit Petrum ab aeterno", et huiusmodi, possunt tamen esse falsae. Et si de facto damnaretur, tunc de facto est falsa vel sunt falsae. Unde ita contingentes sunt cum hac dictione "ab aeterno" sicut sine illa.'
50 *William Ockham*, ed. Adams/Kretzmann, 48–49; ed. Böhner, 516: 'Et dicit Doctor Subtilis quod intellectus divinus, prout quodammodo praecedit determinationem voluntatis divinae, apprehendit illa complexa ut neutra, et voluntas determinat alteram partem esse veram pro aliquo instanti, volens alteram partem esse veram pro eodem instanti. Posita autem determinatione voluntatis, intellectus divinus videt determinationem voluntatis suae quae est immutabilis: videt evidenter alteram partem esse veram, illam scilicet quam voluntas sua vult esse veram certitudinaliter.'
51 See Adams, *William Ockham*, vol. 2, 1137.
52 *William Ockham*, ed. Adams/Kretzmann, 49; ed. Böhner, 517: 'Igitur cum illa determinatio voluntatis non fuit ab aeterno, non habuit Deus certam notitiam illorum.'

past and future present to him. Nevertheless, he acknowledges that we cannot know how God thus knows the future – we can only assume by faith that he does so. As Ockham concludes: 'it is impossible to express clearly the way in which God knows future contingents.'[53]

In a second question, Ockham considers the claim that God has determinate or certain and thus infallible or immutable and necessary knowledge of the truth or falsity of future contingents.[54] Here, Ockham observes that future contingents are not determinately true or false in themselves.[55] Thus, God must know them contingently. In arguing this point, Ockham distinguishes between two ways of understanding the necessity of God's knowledge. The first concerns the nature of God's knowledge of future contingents, which is necessary because God is a necessary being.[56] The second way concerns the nature of the object known, namely, the future contingent, which cannot be known necessarily, even by God, precisely because it is contingent until it actually takes place.[57]

Similar to Scotus, Ockham argues that God's knowledge of the future contingent only becomes necessary when the contingent event occurs. Until then, something God knows to be false could in principle turn out to be true.[58] Although Ockham therefore suggests that God can gain knowledge of something that he did not previously know, he stresses that this does not imply any change in God but only in the creature, which comes into being where it previously did not exist.[59] For Ockham, consequently, God remains in some sense eternal, even though Ockham finally accepts that his knowledge is subject to the temporal categories of past, present, and especially, the future.[60]

---

[53] *William Ockham*, ed. Adams/Kretzmann, 50; ed. Böhner, 517: 'Ideo dico quod impossibile est clare exprimere modum quo Deus scit futura contingentia.'
[54] *William Ockham*, ed. Adams/Kretzmann, 54.
[55] *William Ockham*, ed. Adams/Kretzmann, 54.
[56] *William Ockham*, ed. Adams/Kretzmann, 67; ed. Böhner, 529–30: 'Dico quod hoc potest intelligi dupliciter: uno modo quod scientia Dei qua sciuntur futura contingentia sit necessaria. Et hoc est verum, quia ipsa essentia divina est unica cognitio necessaria et immutabilis omnium tam complexorum quam incomplexorum, necessariorum et contingentium.'
[57] *William Ockham*, ed. Adams/Kretzmann, 67; ed. Böhner, 530: 'Secundo modo, quod per illam scientiam sciantur necessario futura contingentia. Et sic non est necessaria, nec debet concedi quod Deus habeat scientiam necessariam de futuris contingentibus sed potius contingentem, quia sicut hoc futurum contingens contingenter erit, ita Deus scit ipsum contingenter fore, quia potest non scire ipsum fore, si ipsum scit.'
[58] Craig, *The Problem of Divine Foreknowledge*, 154.
[59] *William Ockham*, ed. Adams/Kretzmann, 60.
[60] Craig, *The Problem of Divine Foreknowledge*, 162–3; cf. 167.

In doing so, Ockham arguably articulates a more robust account of God's everlastingness than can be found in the work of earlier Franciscans. As we have seen, the authors of the *Summa Halensis* sought to define God's relationship to time in a way that was compatible with the new tendency to see God as fundamentally infinite and thus intimately, directly related to the movements of finite, temporal beings. For the Summa, this effort involved affirming God's eternity while also rethinking the notion that God knows all things in his 'eternal now'. In place of this, the Summa posited that God is able to conceive of the temporal categories that apply to creatures – especially ones which will come to be in future – which he has caused or will cause.

As noted above, Scotus objected to this view that God knows the future in terms of himself as cause on the grounds that all God's knowledge is necessary – what he knows must come to pass. For this reason, Scotus thinks that positing God's knowledge of the future in the way of the *Summa Halensis* would pre-determine future events and undermine their contingency. In offering his own account of the matter, Scotus argues that God only knows future contingents in virtue of knowing the contents of his will to approve or permit something in the future to occur.

According to Ockham, however, even this prior approval of the divine will would undermine the freedom of the human will and thus the contingency of the future. To circumnavigate the problem, Ockham ultimately declined to explain how God has eternal knowledge of temporal events and denied that he knows what the future holds until it occurs. Whether or not this move had a direct or indirect impact on subsequent thinking, it bears a striking 'family resemblance' to the sort of understanding of God that is quite common today amongst theologians and philosophers of religion who define God as everlasting.[61] To show this, it is worth briefly discussing in closing the way of thinking about God's everlastingness that has been endorsed by many contemporary thinkers. By way of an indicative example, I will consider specifically the account that has been offered by the well-known philosopher Nicholas Wolterstorff, who provides a particularly clear explanation of the reasons why the theory of everlastingness has become so popular in recent times.

---

61 For example, John MacQuarrie, Jürgen Moltmann, Paul Fiddes.

Modern Views of God's Everlasting Nature

In a series of essays, Wolterstorff helpfully explains the key reasons why so many contemporary theologians and philosophers of religion reject the notion that God is timelessly eternal in favor of conceiving him as everlasting. First and foremost, Wolterstorff points out that many scholars, himself to some extent excluded, see the theory of divine timelessness primarily as a product of ancient Greek philosophy, which presented God as a distant and somewhat disinterested or 'impassible' creator whose perfection precludes qualities like temporality that are possessed by natural beings.[62] In the view of many, this account is incompatible with Christian theology and specifically with the way God is portrayed in the Bible, as active in human history and directly involved in human lives.[63]

Although Wolterstorff concedes that God's unchangeability or timelessness is essential to affirming his fidelity to his good purposes, he argues that a distinction can be drawn between God's fidelity to his will for humanity or his redemptive purposes and what might be described as *ontological* unchangeability. According to Wolterstorff, God can be characterized as faithful to his will without being described as fundamentally unchangeable or timeless in his nature. In other words, a change in God's 'time strand' – the unfolding of his orders or will for human beings in time – does not require a change in his essence.[64]

As Wolterstorff admits, Thomas Aquinas might seem to argue along similar lines insofar as he recognizes that 'while God's action existed from all eternity…its existence was not present from eternity, but existed at that time when, from all eternity, He ordained it.'[65] On this account, Wolterstorff elaborates, 'whenever the biblical writers use temporal-event language to describe God's actions, they are to be interpreted as claiming that God acts with respect to some temporal event; they are not to be interpreted as claiming that God's acting is itself a temporal event.'[66] Although Wolterstorff initially entertains Aquinas' theory sympathetically, however, he ultimately declares it unsatisfactory.

The reason he does so is that God in his view cannot know any event has occurred until it has actually taken place – even though he can know that a certain

---

[62] See for example Jürgen Moltmann, *The Crucified God* (London: SCM Press, 1974).
[63] Nicholas Wolterstorff, 'God Everlasting,' in *Inquiring about God: Selected Essays*, vol. 1 (Cambridge: Cambridge University Press, 2010), 133–56. See also Nicholas Wolterstorff, 'Unqualified Divine Temporality,' in *Inquiring about God: Selected Essays*, vol. 1, 157–81.
[64] Nicholas Wolterstorff, 'God Everlasting,' 145.
[65] Nicholas Wolterstorff, 'God Everlasting,' 146.
[66] Nicholas Wolterstorff, 'God Everlasting,' 148.

event *will* occur at a certain time.⁶⁷ As Wolterstorff writes, 'knowing which events occur simultaneously with which falls short of knowing which ones are occurring now.'⁶⁸ As we have seen, Scotus and Ockham made a similar claim, denying that God can know the future until it has come to pass. For these thinkers, the motivation for arguing along these lines was to avoid suggesting that God pre-determines the future and thus undermines free will.

For modern philosophers like Wolterstorff, the aim is more to illustrate how God relates dynamically with human beings in history, identifying with their experiences in time. In that sense, the medieval and the modern thinkers we have considered affirm what seem like similar views at face value for very different reasons. The reasons matter, in that they lead many modern thinkers to go much further than the medieval Franciscans ever did in actually denying that God is outside of time. For many contemporary theologians, in fact, God is subject to temporal categories and constraints, such as the discovery of the future and even the experience of sufferings.⁶⁹

These are conclusions that Franciscan proponents of divine timelessness have wanted to avoid, because they make God seem too much as if he is a 'being like us' rather than a God whose ways are above our own.⁷⁰ In the context of contemporary discussions, consequently, the Franciscan views seemingly offer a valuable resource, in that they affirm that God is outside of time and eternal, even while giving an account of his ability to conceptualize our temporal experiences. The present study has sought to make this resource available by tracing the history of the idea that God is in some sense everlasting to its origins in the early Franciscan school, while elucidating the sources and influences that fostered its development in the work of subsequent Franciscans.

Conclusion

The foregoing study has shown that early Franciscan thinking about God's relationship to time resulted from two fundamental intellectual shifts, one theological, and one more philosophical in nature. The former concerns a tendency to prior-

---

67 Nicholas Wolterstorff, 'God Everlasting,' 150.
68 Nicholas Wolterstorff, 'Unqualified Divine Temporality,' 164.
69 Many modern theologians advocate the idea that God can identify with our sufferings, but a particularly subtle account is offered by Paul Fiddes in *The Creative Suffering of God* (Oxford: Clarendon Press, 1992).
70 See for example Thomas Weinandy's Thomist refutation of claims regarding divine suffering in *Does God Suffer?* (Notre Dame: University of Notre Dame Press, 2000).

itize speaking of God as essentially and primarily infinite, rather than simple, following the inspiration particularly of Richard of St Victor, who already in the twelfth century gestured in the direction of defining God as a being of infinite duration, 'without beginning, end, or change'. The second concerns the appropriation of the metaphysics of Avicenna, in particular, his modal theory, which had implications not only for conceiving God as infinite – and infinite in duration – but also for the Franciscan understanding of time.

As we have seen, followers of Aristotle generally presupposed a 'static' account in which time was conceived as the temporal distance between two points, one before and one after. However, Avicenna took his modal metaphysics as the point of departure for developing a more dynamic view of time. According to this, time is the continuous flow of the 'now' or the present moment from the future into the past, whereby one temporal possibility is realised after another. Thus, Avicenna conceived of time according to an A-series while Aristotle tended to describe time in terms of a B-series.

Although early Franciscans adopted and developed Avicenna's understanding of time, they denied that God himself is subject to the A-series categories of past, present, and future and continued to affirming God's eternity. Nevertheless, the influence of Avicenna had an effect on the way they conceived of God's eternal nature 'from below', just as the doctrine of divine infinity influenced their ideas of his eternity 'from above'. In particular, it encouraged early Franciscans to explain the way in which all times, past, present, and future, are present to God, even while he himself remains atemporal. This is the sense in which I have argued that early Franciscans offered a moderate account of God as an everlasting being, namely, insofar as he knows past, present, and future times as such.

To explain specifically how God knows future possibilities which have not yet been realized, the *Summa Halensis* contends that God knows future events in virtue of knowing himself as the cause of all things. Duns Scotus objected to this view on the grounds that God cannot know what has not yet occurred in time. On his understanding, nothing can be related to God in real terms which does not actually exist. If God were to know the future, Scotus elaborates, then he would pre-determine it, undermining contingency. To circumnavigate this issue, Scotus argued that God knows future contingents by virtue of knowing what he will eventually will or approve or bring about.

Ockham objected to this view on the grounds that even God's foreknowledge of his own will would pre-determine the future and undermine human free will. As a result, Ockham concluded that God cannot know the future – or at least we cannot know how he knows it – until it actually comes about. Although Ockham continued to affirm that God is in some sense eternal, consequently, he resorted in practice to describing God as everlasting and thereby crystallized the Franciscan move in the direction of this doctrine. As we have seen, the alternative that was favoured by earlier medieval thinkers as well as Aquinas in the thirteenth century was the traditional doctrine of God as timelessly eternal, which affirmed that God knows all times as present in his 'eternal now'.

Both the Franciscan account as well as the idea that God is timelessly eternal arguably affirm the transcendence of God and his ability to engage with or conceptualize immanent creatures. Nevertheless, eternalism lay the emphasis on God's otherness while the doctrine of everlastingness stresses the relation of all times to him. As noted above, these differences in emphasis in terms of God's relation to time follow from a deeper difference in understanding the nature of God and his relationship to creatures: either as simple and thus incommensurable with finite beings or as infinite and thus directly related to finite beings as their cause, while nonetheless superseding them. Each approach to understanding God – as simple/eternal or infinite/everlasting – therefore forms an organic and internally coherent whole, with its own theological strengths and priorities.

This work has sought to offer an historical recounting of the development of the two accounts and in particular the medieval Franciscan way of thinking about God as everlasting, which was novel in the Latin tradition in its own time. Although the later Franciscan views particularly bear some resemblance to modern accounts of God's everlastingness, many of these go much further in attributing temporal categories to God, which might ultimately seem unbefitting of his supreme nature. In this context, I have sought to recover a more moderate approach to think of God's everlasting nature which can be found in the work of early Franciscan authors. By making this resource available, this work gives pause to consider the respects in which God can legitimately be described as *both* eternal *and* everlasting, opening doors for a broader conception of the divine being whose greatness and power is beyond anything that our minds can actually contain.

Bibliography

Primary Sources

Alan of Lille. 'La Somme Quoniam Homines d'Alain de Lille,' edited by Palémon Glorieux. *Archives d'histoire doctrinale et littéraire du Moyen Âge* 20 (1953), 113–364.

Alexander of Hales. *Magistri Alexandri de Hales Glossa in quatuor libros Sententiarum Petri Lombardi*, vol. 1. Florence: Collegii S. Bonaventurae, 1951.

Alexander of Hales. *Quaestiones disputatae quae ad rerum universitatem pertinent*, edited by Jacek Mateusz Wierzbicki. Grottaferrata: Collegii S. Bonaventurae, 2013.

Anselm of Canterbury. *Anselm of Canterbury: The Major Works*, edited by Brian Davies, Gillian R. Evans. Oxford: Oxford University Press, 2008.

Aristotle. *Physics Books III and IV*, translated by Edward Hussey. Oxford: Clarendon Press, 1983.

Augustine. *The City of God Books VIII-XVI*, translated by Gerald G. Walsh, Grace Monahan. In *The Fathers of The Church*, vol. 14. Washington, D.C.: The Catholic University of America Press, 1952.

Augustine. *The City of God I-VII*, translated by Demetrius B. Zema, Gerald G. Walsh. In *The Fathers of The Church*, vol. 8. Washington, D.C.: The Catholic University of America Press, 1950.

Augustine. *The Trinity*, translated by Stephen McKenna. In *The Fathers of The Church*, vol. 45. Washington, D.C.: The Catholic University of America Press, 1963.

Augustine. *Confessions*, translated by Vernon J. Bourke. In *The Fathers of The Church*, vol. 21. Washington, D.C.: The Catholic University of America Press, 1953.

Augustine. *De diversis quaestionibus ad Simplicianum*, edited by Almut Mutzenbecher. In Corpus Christianorum, Series Latina, vol. 44. Turnhout: Brepols, 1970.

Avicenna. *Metaphysics*. In *Avicenna Latinus: Liber de Philosophia Prima sive Scientia Divina*, vol. 1, edited by Simone Van Riet. Leiden: Brill, 1977.

Avicenna. *The Metaphysics of the Healing*, translated by Michael E. Marmura. Provo: Brigham Young University Press, 2005.

Avicenna. *The Physics of the Healing*, translated by Jon McGinnis. Provo: Brigham Young University Press, 2009.

Augustine. *Eighty-three Different Questions*, translated by David L. Mosher. In *The Fathers of The Church*, vol. 70. Washington, D.C.: The Catholic University of America Press, 2010.

Augustine. *On the Free Choice of the Will*, translated by Peter King. Cambridge: Cambridge University Press, 2010.

Boethius. *Theological Tractates. The Consolation of Philosophy*, translated by Hugh F. Stewart, Edward K. Rand, S. Jim Tester. Loeb Classical Library 74. Cambridge, MA: Harvard University Press, 1973.

Boethius. *The Consolation of Philosophy*, translated by David R. Slavitt. Cambridge, MA: Harvard University Press, 2008.

Bonaventure. *In librum primum Sententiarum*. In *Opera omnia*, Tome 2. Paris: Vivès, 1864.

Bonaventure. *Commentary on the Sentences: Philosophy of God, Sententiae*, translated by Richard E. Houser, Timothy B. Noone. St Bonaventure, NY: The Franciscan Institute, 2014.

Hilary of Poitiers. *De Trinitate*. In *Sancti Hilarii Pictaviensis Episcopi De Trinitate Libri*, edited by Hugo Hurter. Oeniponti: Libraria Academica Wagneriana, 1887.

Hilary of Poitiers. *Saint Hilary of Poitiers: The Trinity,* translated by Stephen McKenna. In *The Fathers of the Church*, vol. 25. Washington, D.C.: The Catholic University of America Press, 1954.
John Duns Scotus. *Questions Subtilissimae super libros metaphysicorum Aristotelis.* In *Opera Omnia,* vol. 7, edited by Luke Wadding. Paris: Vivès, 1891.
John Duns Scotus. *Opus Oxoniense (Ordinatio).* In *Opera omnia,* vol. 6, edited by Karl Balić. Civitas Vaticana: Typis Polyglottia Vaticanis, 1963.
John Duns Scotus. *Ordinatio, Liber Secundus I-3.* In *Opera omnia,* vol. 7, edited by Karl Balić. Civitas Vaticana: Typos Polyglottis Vaticanis: 1973.
John Duns Scotus. *The Examined Report of the Paris Lecture (Reportatio I-A),* vol. 2, edited and translated by Allan B. Wolter, Oleg V. Bychkov. St Bonaventure, NY: Franciscan Institute Publications, 2008.
John Duns Scotus. *Contingency and Freedom, Lectura I 39,* edited and translated by Antoine Vos, Henri Veldhuis, Aline H. Looman-Graanskamp, Eef Dekker, Nico W. den Bok. Dordrecht: Kluwer Academic Publishers, 1994.
John Duns Scotus. *Duns Scotus on Time and Existence: The Questions on Aristotle's "De interpretatione",* edited and translated with introduction and commentary by Edward Buchner, Jack Zupko. Washington, DC: The Catholic University of America Press, 2014.
John Duns Scotus. *God and Creatures: The Quodlibetal Questions,* edited by Felix Alluntis, Allan B. Wolter. Princeton: Princeton University Press, 1975.
Peter John Olivi. *Quodlibeta Quinque,* edited by Stephanus Defraia. Grottaferrata: Collegii S. Bonaventurae, 2002.
Peter Lombard. *Magistri Petri Lombardi Parisiensis episcopi Sententiae in IV libris distinctae*, vol. 1. Grottaferrata: Collegii S. Bonaventurae Ad Claras Aquas, 1971.
Peter Lombard. *The Sentences: Book 1,* translated by Giulio Silano. Toronto: Pontifical Institute of Medieval Studies, 2007.
Richard of Mediavilla. *Super Quatuor Libros Sententiarum, Tomus Secundus.* Brixiae, 1591.
Richard of St Victor. *De Trinitate: texte critique avec introduction, notes et tables*, edited by Jean Ribaillier. Paris: J. Vrin, 1958.
Richard of St Victor. *Richard of St Victor: On the Trinity,* translated by Ruben Angelici. Eugene: Cascade Books, 2011.
Summa Halensis. Doctoris irrefragabilis Alexandri de Hales Ordinis minorum Summa theologica, 4 vols. Quaracchi, Florentiae: Collegii S. Bonaventurae, 1924–48.
Summa Halensis. In *A Reader in Early Franciscan Theology: The Summa Halensis,* edited and translated by Oleg V. Bychkov, Lydia Schumacher. Fordham: Fordham University Press, 2022.
Vital du Four. *Vitalis de Furno, Quodlibeta Tria,* edited by Ferdinand M. Delorme O.F.M. Rome: Antonianum, 1947.
William of Ockham. *Tractatus de praedestinatione et de praescientia Dei respectu futurorum contingentium.* In *Opera Philosophica et Theologica*, vol. 1/2, edited by Philotheus Böhner. St Bonaventure, NY: The Franciscan Institute, 1978.
William of Ockham. *Quaestiones in Librum secundum Sententiarum (Reportatio).* In *Guillelmi de Ockham, Opera Theologica*, vol. 5, edited by Gédeon Gal, Rega Wood. St Bonaventure, NY: Franciscan Institute Press, 1981.
William of Ockham. *Brevis Summa Libri Physicorum, Summula Philosophiae Naturalis et Quaestiones in Libros Physicorum Aristoteles.* In *Opera Philosophica*, vol. 6, edited by Stephen Brown. St Bonaventure, NY: Franciscan Institute Press, 1984.

William of Ockham. *Expositio in Libros Physicorum Aristoteles, Libri IV-VIII*, edited by Vladimir Richer, Gerhard Leibold, Rega Wood St Bonaventure, NY: Franciscan Institute Press, 1985.

William of Ockham. *William Ockham: Predestination, God's Foreknowledge, and Future Contingents*, translated by Marilyn McCord Adams, Norman Kretzmann. Indianapolis: Hackett, 1983.

Secondary Sources

Adams, Marilyn McCord. *William Ockham*, vol. 2. Notre Dame: University of Notre Dame Press, 1987.

Amichay, Suf. 'Freedom and Plenitude in Medieval Arguments for the Existence of God.' PhD: Cambridge University, 2023.

Arif, Syamsuddin. 'Neither Created nor Destructible: Ibn Sīnā on the Eternity of the Universe.' *Al-Shajarah: ISTAC Journal of Islamic Thought and Civilization* 25:1 (2020), 85–106.

Bertolacci, Amos. 'On the Latin Reception of Avicenna's Metaphysics before Albertus Magnus: An Attempt at Periodization.' In *The Arabic, Hebrew and Latin Reception of Avicenna's Metaphysics*, edited by Dag Nikolaus Hasse, Amos Bertolacci, 197–223. Berlin: De Gruyter, 2012.

Bertolacci, Amos. 'Reading Aristotle with Avicenna: On the Reception of the *Philosophia Prima* in the *Summa Halensis*.' In *The Summa Halensis: Sources and Context*, edited by Lydia Schumacher, 135–54. Berlin: De Gruyter, 2020.

Bianchi, Luca. *L'errore di Aristotele: la polemica contro l'eternità del mondo nel XIII secolo*. Florence: La Nuova Italia, 1984.

Bianchi, Luca. *L'inizio dei tempi: antichità e novità del mondo da Bonaventura a Newton*. Florence: Olschki, 1987.

Bieniak, Magdalena. *The Body-Soul Problem at Paris ca. 1200–1250*. Leuven: Leuven University Press, 2010.

Boulnois, Olivier. 'Du temps cosmique à la durée ontologique? Duns Scot, le temps, l'album et l'éternité.' In *The Medieval Concept of Time*, edited by Pasquale Porro, 161–88. Leiden: Brill, 2001.

Burr, David. *Olivi and Franciscan Poverty: The Origins of the 'Usus Pauper' Controversy*. Philadelphia: University of Pennsylvania Press, 1989.

Coope, Ursula. *Time for Aristotle: Physics IV.10–14*. Oxford: Clarendon Press, 2005.

Colish, Marcia L. *Peter Lombard*, 2 vols. Leiden: Brill, 1993.

Côté, Antoine. *L'infinité divine dans la théologie médiévale (1220–1255)*. Paris: Vrin, 2002.

Courtenay, William J. *Capacity and Volition: A History of the Distinction of Absolute and Ordained Power*. Bergamo: Pierluigi Lubrina, 1990.

Craig, William Lane. *The Problem of Divine Foreknowledge and Future Contingents from Aristotle to Suarez*. Leiden: Brill, 1988.

Craig, William Lane. 'The Tensed vs. Tenseless Theory of Time: A Watershed for the Conception of Divine Eternity.' In *Questions of Time and Tense*, edited by Robin Le Poidevin, 221–50. Oxford: Oxford University Press, 1998.

Craig, William Lane. 'John Duns Scotus on God's Foreknowledge and Future Contingents.' *Franciscan Studies* 47 (1987), 98–122.

Cross, Richard. 'Duns Scotus on Eternity and Timelessness.' *Faith and Philosophy* 14:1 (1992), 3–25.

Cross, Richard. *The Physics of Duns Scotus: The Scientific Context of a Theological Vision*. Oxford: Oxford University Press, 1998.

Cross, Richard. 'Angelic Time and Motion: Bonaventure to Duns Scotus.' In *A Companion to Angels in Medieval Philosophy,* edited by Tobias Hoffmann, 117–47. Leiden: Brill, 2012.
Dales, Richard C. *Medieval Discussions of the Eternity of the World.* Leiden: Brill, 1990.
Dales, Richard C. 'Time and Eternity in the Thirteenth Century.' *Journal of the History of Ideas* 49:1 (Jan–Mar 1988), 27–45.
Davidson, Herbert Alan. *Proofs for Eternity, Creation, and the Existence of God in Medieval Islamic and Jewish Philosophy.* Oxford: Oxford University Press, 1987.
Davenport, Anne Ashley. *Measure of a Different Greatness: The Intensive Infinite, 1250–1650.* Leiden: Brill, 1999.
Denifle, Heinrich, ed. *Chartularium Universitatis Parisiensis* I. Paris: Fratre Delalain, 1899 (repr. Bruxelles, 1964).
Dondaine, Hyacinthe-François. 'L'objet et le "medium" de la vision béatifique chez les théologiens du XIIIe siècle.' *Recherches de théologie ancienne et médiévale* 19 (1952), 60–130.
Fiddes, Paul. *The Creative Suffering of God.* Oxford: Clarendon Press, 1992.
Flasch, Kurt. *Was ist Zeit? Augustinus von Hippo. Das XI. Buch der Confessiones.* Frankfurt am Main: Klostermann, 2004.
Frost, Gloria. 'John Duns Scotus on God's Knowledge of Sins: A Test-Case for God's Knowledge of Contingents.' *Journal of the History of Philosophy* 48:1 (2010), 15–34.
Frost, Gloria. 'Divine Power, Knowledge and Will.' In *The Oxford Handbook of Medieval Franciscan Thought,* edited by Drew Rosato, Lydia Schumacher. Oxford: Oxford University Press, forthcoming.
Hasse, Dag Nikolaus. *Avicenna's De anima in the Latin West: The Formation of a Peripatetic Philosophy of the Soul 1160–1300.* London: The Warburg Institute, 2000.
Henninger, Mark G. *Relations: Medieval Theories 1250–1325.* Oxford: Clarendon Press, 1989.
Hintikka Jaakko. 'Necessity, Universality and Time in Aristotle.' *Ajatus* 20 (1957), 65–90.
Hoenen, Maarten J.F.M. 'Scotus and the Scotist School: The Tradition of Scotist Thought in the Medieval and Early Modern Period.' In *John Duns Scotus (1265/6–1308): Renewal of Philosophy,* edited by Egbert P. Bos, 197–210. Amsterdam: Rodopi, 1998.
Janssens, Jules. 'What about Providence and the Best of All Possible Worlds? Avicenna and Leibniz.' In *Fate, Providence and Moral Responsibility in Ancient, Medieval and Early Modern Thought,* edited by Peter d'Hoine, Gerd Van Riel, 441–54. Leuven: Leuven University Press, 2014.
Jeck, Udo Reinhold. *Aristoteles contra Augustinum. Zur Frage nach dem Verhältnis von Zeit und Seele bei den antiken Aristoteleskommentatoren, im arabischen Aristotelismus und im 13. Jahrhundert.* Amsterdam: B.R. Grüner, 1994.
Jordan, Robert. 'Time and Contingency in Augustine.' *The Review of Metaphysics* 8:3 (1995), 394–417.
Kaukua, Jari. 'Future Contingency and God's Knowledge of Particulars in Avicenna.' *British Journal for the History of Philosophy* (published online 2022), 1–21.
Knuuttila, Simo. 'Time and Creation in Augustine.' In *The Cambridge Companion to Augustine,* edited by David V. Meconi, Eleonore Stump, 81–97. Cambridge: Cambridge University Press, 2014.
Knuuttila, Simo. *Modalities in Medieval Philosophy.* London: Routledge, 2020.
Knuuttila, Simo, Gloria Frost. 'Medieval Theories of Future Contingents.' *Stanford Encyclopedia of Philosophy,* https://plato.stanford.edu/archives/sum2025/entries/medieval-futcont, accessed 1 March 2025.
Kolbinger, Florian. *Zeit und Ewigkeit. Philosophisch-theologische Beiträge Bonaventuras zum Diskurs des 13. Jahrhunderts um* tempus *und* aevum. Berlin: De Gruyter, 2014.

Leftow, Brian. *Time and Eternity*. Ithaca: Cornell University Press, 2009.
Maier, Anneliese. 'Die Subjektivierung der Zeit in der scholastischen Philosophie.' *Philosophia naturalis* 1 (1951), 361–96.
Marmura, Michael E. 'Divine Omniscience and Future Contingents in Alfarabi and Avicenna.' In *Divine Omniscience and Omnipotence in Medieval Philosophy*, edited by Tamar Rudavsky, 81–94. Dordrecht: Reidel, 1985.
McGinnis, Jon. 'Time and Time Again: A Study of Aristotle and Ibn Sina's Temporal Theories.' PhD: University of Pennsylvania, 2000.
McGinnis, Jon. 'The Topology of Time: An Analysis of Medieval Islamic Accounts of Discrete and Continuous Time.' *The Modern Schoolman* 81 (2003), 5–25.
McGinnis, Jon. 'Time to Change: Time, Motion and Possibility in Ibn Sīnā.' In *Uluslararası İbn Sînâ Sempozyumu Bildiriler*, vol. 1, edited by Mehmet Mazak, Nevzat Özkaya, 251–57. Istanbul: Istanbul Büyükşehır Belediyesi, 2008.
McGinnis, Jon. *Avicenna*. Oxford: Oxford University Press, 2010.
McGinnis, Jon. 'Avicennan Infinity: A Select History of the Infinite through Avicenna.' *Documenti e Studi sulla tradizione filosofica medievale* 21 (2010), 199–222.
McGinnis, Jon. 'The Ultimate Why Question: Avicenna on Why God is Absolutely Necessary.' In *The Ultimate Why Question: Why is There Anything at All Rather Than Nothing Whatsoever?*, edited by John Wippel, 65–83. Washington, D.C.: Catholic University Press, 2011.
McGinnis, Jon. 'Creation and Eternity in Medieval Philosophy.' In *A Companion to the Philosophy of Time*, edited by Adrian Bardon, Heather Dyke, 73–86. Oxford: John Wiley & Sons, 2013.
McGinnis, Jon. 'The Eternity of the World: Proofs and Problems in Aristotle, Avicenna, and Aquinas.' *American Catholic Philosophical Quarterly* (2014), 1–19.
McTaggart, John M. Ellis. 'The Unreality of Time.' *Mind* 689 (1908), 457–74.
McTaggart, John M. Ellis. *The Nature of Existence*, vol. 2. Cambridge: Cambridge University Press, 1927.
Moltmann, Jürgen. *The Crucified God*. London: SCM Press, 1974.
Mullins, Ryan T. *The End of the Timeless God*. Oxford: Oxford University Press, 2016.
Normore, Calvin. 'Future Contingents.' In *The Cambridge History of Later Medieval Philosophy*, edited by Norman Kretzmann, Anthony Kenny, Jan Pinborg, Eleonore Stump, 358–81. Cambridge: Cambridge University Press, 1982.
Porro, Pasquale. *Forme E Modelli Di Durata Nel Pensiero Medievale: L'Aevum, Il Tempo Discreto, La Categoria 'Quando'*. Leuven: Leuven University Press, 1996.
Porro, Pasquale. 'Angelic Measures: *Aevum* and Discrete Time.' In *The Medieval Concept of Time: Studies on the Scholastic Debate and its Reception in Early Modern Philosophy*, edited by Pasquale Porro, 131–59. Leiden: Brill, 2001.
Rosemann, Philipp W. *Peter Lombard*. Oxford: Oxford University Press, 2004.
Rosemann, Philipp W. *The Story of a Great Medieval Book: Peter Lombard's Sentences*. Toronto: University of Toronto Press, 2007.
Rosheger, John P. 'Augustine and Divine Simplicity.' *New Blackfriars* 77:901 (February 1996), 72–83.
Schmutz, Jacob. 'L'héritage des subtils: cartographie du Scotisme de l'âge classique.' *Les études philosophiques* 60 (2002), 51–81.
Schumacher, Lydia. 'The Early Franciscan Doctrine of Divine Immensity: Towards a Middle Way Between Classical Theism and Panentheism.' *Scottish Journal of Theology* 70:3 (2017), 278–94.
Schumacher, Lydia. *Early Franciscan Theology: Between Authority and Innovation*. Cambridge: Cambridge University Press, 2019.

Schumacher, Lydia. 'The *De anima* Tradition in Early Franciscan Thought: A Case Study in Avicenna's Reception.' *Mediaevalia* 38 (2019), 97–115.
Schumacher, Lydia. 'Christian Platonism in the Medieval West.' In *Christian Platonism: A History*, 183–206. Cambridge: Cambridge University Press, 2020.
Schumacher, Lydia. 'The Proof for a Necessary Existent in the *Summa Halensis*.' In *The Summa Halensis: Doctrines and Debates*, edited by Lydia Schumacher, 59–72. Berlin: De Gruyter, 2020.
Schumacher, Lydia. 'Rethinking the Reception of Augustine in Early Franciscan Psychology (c. 1230–45).' *Cithara* 60:2 (May 2021), 3–16.
Schumacher, Lydia. 'The Divine Ideas in the Early Franciscan School at Paris (c. 1220–50).' In *Theories of Divine Ideas: From the Church Fathers to the Early Franciscan Masters*, edited by Tommaso Manzon, Irene Zavattero, 237–59. Rome: Aracne, 2023.
Schumacher, Lydia. *Human Nature in Early Franciscan Thought: Philosophical Background and Theological Significance.* Cambridge: Cambridge University Press, 2023.
Schumacher, Lydia. 'Divine Power and Possible Worlds in Early Franciscan Thought: A Case Study in Avicenna's Reception.' In *Religionsdialoge und Wissensordnungen*, edited by Alexander Fidora, Matthias Lutz-Bachmann. Tübingen: Mohr Siebeck, forthcoming.
Schumacher, Lydia. 'The Divine Nature.' In *The Origins of Scholasticism: Theology and Philosophy in Paris 1150–1250*, edited by Lydia Schumacher, 183–207. Cambridge: Cambridge University Press, 2025.
Shapiro, Herman. *Motion, Time and Space According to William Ockham.* St Bonaventure, N. Y., The Franciscan Institute, 1957.
Söder, Joachim Roland. *Kontingenz und Wissen. Die Lehre von den* futura contingentia *bei Johannes Duns Scotus.* Münster: Aschendorff Verlag, 1999.
Sorabji, Richard. *Time, Creation and the Continuum: Theories in Antiquity and the Early Middle Ages.* London: Duckworth, 1983.
Spatz, Nancy. 'Approaches and Attitudes to a New Theology Textbook: The *Sentences* of Peter Lombard.' In *The Intellectual Climate of the Early University: Essays in Honor of Otto Gründler*, edited by Nancy van Deusen, 27–52. Kalamazoo: Medieval Institute Publications, Western Michigan University, 1997.
Stump, Eleonore, Norman Kretzmann. 'Eternity.' *The Journal of Philosophy* 78:8 (August 1981), 429–58.
Swinburne, Richard. *The Coherence of Theism.* Oxford: Clarendon Press, 1977.
Suarez-Nani, Tiziana. 'On Divine Immensity and Infinity in Relation to Space and Time: The Crossroad of the *Summa Halensis*.' In *The Legacy of Early Franciscan Thought,* edited by Lydia Schumacher, 71–87. Berlin: De Gruyter, 2021.
Sweeney, Leo S.J. 'Divine Infinity: 1150–1250.' *The Modern Schoolman* 35 (November 1957), 38–51.
Tomkinson, John L. 'Divine Sempiternity and Atemporality.' *Religious Studies* 18 (1982), 177–89.
Toth, Zita. 'Creation.' In *The Origins of Scholasticism: Philosophy and Theology in Paris 1150–1250*, edited by Lydia Schumacher, 237–59. Cambridge: Cambridge University Press, 2025.
Ward, Keith. *God: A Guide for the Perplexed.* London: OneWorld Publishers, 2002.
Weinandy, Thomas. *Does God Suffer?* Notre Dame: University of Notre Dame Press, 2000.
Wisnovsky, Robert. 'One Aspect of the Avicennian Turn in Sunnī Theology.' *Arabic Sciences and Philosophy* 14 (2004), 65–100.
Wolter, Allan B. 'Scotus' Paris Lectures on God's Knowledge of Future Events.' In *The Philosophical Theology of John Duns Scotus*, edited by Marilyn McCord Adams, Allan B. Wolter, 285–333. Ithaca: Cornell, 1990.

Wolterstorff, Nicholas. 'Unqualified Divine Temporality.' In *Inquiring about God: Selected Essays*, vol. 1, 157–81. Cambridge: Cambridge University Press, 2010.

Wolterstorff, Nicholas. 'God Everlasting.' In *Inquiring about God: Selected Essays*, vol. 1, 133–56. Cambridge: Cambridge University Press, 2010.

Wood, Jacob W. 'Kataphasis and Apophasis in Thirteenth Century Theology: The Anthropological Context of the *Triplex Via* in the *Summa fratris Alexandri* and Albert the Great.' *The Heythrop Journal* 57 (2016), 293–311.

Zachhuber, Johannes. *Time and the Soul from Aristotle to St Augustine*. Berlin: De Gruyter, 2022.

Index of Names

Alan of Lille   7–8, 16–17, 19, 22, 30
Alexander of Hales   2, 8, 11, 13, 17–19, 22, 32–34, 36, 38, 43, 51, 53, 61–62, 87
Anselm of Canterbury   1, 3, 7–8, 10, 16, 22, 28–30, 34, 37, 43, 49
Aristotle   2, 4, 20–21, 24–25, 39–41, 47, 49–51, 54–56, 61–62, 65–70, 72–74, 76–82, 84, 100, 111
Augustine   1, 3, 7–9, 11–12, 22–26, 29, 34, 39, 49, 56, 60–61, 67, 72–73, 84, 92, 111
Averroes   2, 23, 66–67, 72
Avicenna   2–4, 14, 20–22, 36, 39–50, 54–62, 75, 80–82, 84, 100

Boethius   1, 3, 7–10, 22, 26–30, 34, 49, 60–61, 84, 86
Bonaventure   36, 52, 63, 66, 76, 86, 91, 94

Francis of Assisi   1

Gundissalinus, Dominicus   14

Henry of Ghent   91, 93
Hilary of Poitiers   7, 11–13
Hugh of St Victor   13

Isidore of Seville   19

John Duns Scotus   4–5, 66–70, 76, 81, 83, 87–97, 99–100
John of Damascus   3, 7, 20
John of La Rochelle   2, 8, 18–19, 35
John Scotus Eriugena   14

McTaggart, John M. Ellis   4, 49

Ockham, William of   4–5, 47, 66–67, 76–80, 82–83, 87, 94–97, 99–100

Peter John Olivi   66, 70–73
Peter Lombard   8, 11–13, 16, 18, 22, 30–34, 86
Pseudo-Dionysius   3, 7, 13, 20

Richard of Middleton   66, 74, 82
Richard of St Victor   3, 7–8, 13–16, 22, 35, 100

Summa Halensis   2–4, 8, 11, 13–22, 35–40, 42–53, 60–66, 69, 80–81, 83–87, 97, 100

Thomas Aquinas   2, 8, 23, 52, 62–63, 89, 91–93, 98, 101

Vital du Four   66, 73–74, 81

Index of Subjects

Accidents 9, 12, 18, 32 – 33, 42, 44, 64, 69
aevum 23, 36, 60 – 61, 63 – 64, 67, 71
analogy 36, 42, 44, 55, 62, 81
angel(s) 35, 48, 60 – 61, 63 – 64, 68, 74
Aristotelian categories 9
A-series (of time) 4, 49, 92, 100
Attributes (of God) 9 – 10, 13, 15 – 16, 43

Benedictine (order) 10
B-series (of time) 4, 92, 100

complexa 90, 93 – 95
Contingent/contingency 4 – 5, 28 – 29, 34, 89 – 90, 97, 100
– See future contingents 4 – 5, 33, 46, 54, 84 – 85, 87 – 91, 93 – 94, 96 – 97, 100
Continuous/discrete (time) 62 – 66, 73 – 75, 77 – 78, 80 – 82

Dominican order 2, 23, 62 – 63

Eternal (God) 1 – 3, 5 – 6, 8, 12, 14 – 15, 17, 22, 25 – 29, 31 – 33, 35 – 36, 38, 48, 50 – 51, 59 – 61, 65, 82, 84 – 87, 91 – 93, 96 – 101
'eternal now' 4, 15, 22, 25 – 26, 33 – 34, 66, 82, 91 – 92, 97, 101
Eternity of the world 49 – 53, 65
Everlasting(ness) of God 1 – 6, 8, 15, 22, 35, 38 – 39, 48, 51, 54, 59 – 60, 66, 82, 87, 93, 97 – 101
– 'flowing now' 56, 58, 68, 71, 77, 80 – 82

Foreknowledge, divine 5, 25 – 27, 29, 30 – 31, 33 – 34, 84 – 87, 95, 100
Franciscan order 1 – 6, 18, 34, 51, 66, 80 – 83, 99 – 101
Freedom of the will/free will 5, 26, 28 – 29, 34, 86, 89, 94 – 95, 97, 99 – 100
Future contingents 4 – 5, 25, 33, 46, 54, 84, 87 – 91, 93 – 94, 96 – 97, 100

Ideas, divine 38, 89, 91
Immensity, divine 13, 17, 19, 89, 91
Immutability, divine 8, 15, 17, 24, 29, 31, 34 – 36, 68, 81, 90, 95,

Infallibility (of God) 31, 86, 88, 96
Infinite worlds 47
Infinity, divine 2 – 5, 7 – 8, 13 – 22, 35, 37 – 38, 40, 43 – 48, 63, 83, 92 – 93, 97, 100 – 101

Metaphysics 2, 14, 20, 23, 39 – 42, 44 – 50, 54, 68 – 69, 81, 100
Modal metaphysics 40, 42, 45, 48 – 50, 54, 58 – 59, 100
Motion 4, 24, 30, 50 – 51, 54 – 64, 66, 68 – 83

Necessary being/existent 14, 21, 36 – 37, 40 – 43, 45, 48 – 50, 59 – 60. 96
Neo-Platonism 3, 39

Objective/subjective existence time (outside the soul) 23, 55, 66, 71 – 73, 79, 81

Paris University 16, 18, 66
Possible being 3, 40 – 41, 43, 45, 47, 60
Possible worlds 39 – 40, 45 – 47
Providence 45 – 46

Sempiternity/sempiternal 27, 35 – 36, 48, 60,
Sentences of Peter Lombard 11, 18, 30, 68, 76 – 79
Simplicity, divine 3, 7 – 13, 16 – 19, 22, 32, 68, 100 – 101
Statistical/temporal frequency model of time 40 – 41, 55
Substance 9 – 10, 20, 32 – 33, 35, 42, 44, 46, 51 – 53, 60 – 61, 63, 68 – 70, 81

Time 1 – 6, 9, 12 – 13, 15, 17, 19 – 25, 27 – 30, 33 – 41, 47 – 51, 54 – 84, 87, 89 – 93, 97 – 101, 111 – 12
– Dynamic theory 4, 49, 56, 58, 61, 80, 81, 83, 100
– Static theory 4, 24, 55 – 56, 80, 82, 100
Trinity 11, 13, 19, 52

Univocal/univocity 40, 42, 44

Will, divine 5, 90, 94, 95, 97

The following volumes have been published in this series:

Volume 2
Detel, Wolfgang. *Subjektive und objektive Zeit: Aristoteles und die moderne Zeit-Theorie.* Berlin/Boston: De Gruyter, 2021.

Volume 3
Singer, P. N. *Time for the Ancients: Measurement, Theory, Experience.* Berlin/Boston: De Gruyter, 2022.

Volume 4
Gertzen, Thomas L. *Aber die Zeit fürchtet die Pyramiden: Die Wissenschaften vom Alten Orient und die zeitliche Dimension von Kulturgeschichte.* Berlin/Boston: De Gruyter, 2022.

Volume 6
Zachhuber, Johannes. *Time and Soul: From Aristotle to St. Augustine.* Berlin/Boston: De Gruyter, 2022.

Volume 7
Golitsis, Pantelis. *Damascius' Philosophy of Time.* Berlin/Boston: De Gruyter, 2023.

Volume 8
Defaux, Olivier. *La Table des rois: Contribution à l'histoire textuelle des ›Tables faciles‹ de Ptolémée.* Berlin/Boston: De Gruyter, 2023.

Volume 9
Fischer, Julia (ed.). *Zwiegespräche über die Zeit: Dialoge in der Berlin-Brandenburgischen Akademie der Wissenschaften aus Anlass des sechzigsten Geburtstags von Christoph Markschies.* Berlin/Boston: De Gruyter, 2024.

Volume 10
Walter, Anke (ed.). *The Temporality of Festivals: Approaches to Festive Time in Ancient Babylon, Greece, Rome, and Medieval China.* Berlin/Boston: De Gruyter, 2024.

Volume 12
Sieroka, Norman. *Zeit-Hören: Erfahrungen, Taktungen, Musik.* Berlin/Boston: De Gruyter, 2024.

Volume 13
Birk, Ralph/Coulon, Laurent (eds.). *The Thebaid in Times of Crisis: Revolt and Response in Ptolemaic Egypt.* Berlin/Boston: De Gruyter, 2025.

Volume 14
Pallavidini, Marta. *(A)synchronic (Re)actions: Crises and Their Perception in Hittite History.* Berlin/Boston: De Gruyter, 2025.

Volume 15
Nosch, Marie-Louise Bech. *Time and Textiles in Ancient Greece.* Berlin/Boston: De Gruyter, 2025.

Volume 16
Klinger, Jörg. *Das Erfassen von Zeit im Kontext der Vergangenheit.* Berlin/Boston: De Gruyter, 2026.

Volume 17
Zachhuber, Johannes. *Time and History in Denis Pétau. Philosophy, Science, and Religion in Early Modern France.* Berlin/Boston: De Gruyter, 2026.

Volume 18
Ossendrijver, Mathieu. *Conceptions of Cyclicity in Babylonian and Greco-Roman Scholarship.* Berlin/Boston: De Gruyter, 2025.

www.ingramcontent.com/pod-product-compliance
Lightning Source LLC
Chambersburg PA
CBHW070317240426
43661CB00057B/2672